The Best of /AIXtra

An Eclectic UNIX Anthology, Volume III

Alan E. Hodel

For book and bookstore information

http://www.prenhall.com

Prentice Hall P T R
Upper Saddle River, NJ 07458

Library of Congress Cataloging-in-Publication Data

The Best of /AIXtra [sic] : an eclectic UNIX anthology / [edited by]
    Alan E. Hodel.
        p. cm.
    Includes index.
    ISBN 0-13-328626-6
    1. UNIX (Computer file) 2. Operating systems (Computers)
I. Hodel, Alan E. II. AIXtra.
QA76.76.063B475   1995
005.4'469--dc20   95-32188
                                                             CIP

Editorial/production supervision: *Jane Bonnell*
Manufacturing manager: *Alexis R. Heydt*
Acquisitions editor: *Mike Meehan*
Cover design director: *Jerry Votta*

©1997 by International Business Machines Corporation

Published by Prentice Hall PTR
Prentice-Hall, Inc.
A Simon & Schuster Company
Upper Saddle River, NJ 07458

The publisher offers discounts on this book when ordered in bulk quantities.
For more information, contact:

    Corporate Sales Department
    Prentice Hall PTR
    One Lake Street
    Upper Saddle River, NJ 07458
    Phone: 800-382-3419
    Fax: 201-236-7141
    e-mail: corpsales@prenhall.com

Printed in the United States of America
10 9 8 7 6 5 4 3 2 1

ISBN   0-13-494444-5

Prentice-Hall International (UK) Limited, *London*
Prentice-Hall of Australia Pty. Limited, *Sydney*
Prentice-Hall Canada Inc., *Toronto*
Prentice-Hall Hispanoamericana, S.A., *Mexico*
Prentice-Hall of India Private Limited, *New Delhi*
Prentice-Hall of Japan, Inc., *Tokyo*
Simon & Schuster Asia Pte. Ltd., *Singapore*
Editora Prentice-Hall do Brasil, Ltda., *Rio de Janeiro*

The Best of /AIXtra

An Eclectic UNIX Anthology, Volume III

TECHNOLOGY TRENDS

The Best of /AIXtra

An Eclectic UNIX Anthology, Volume III

Acknowledgements

Introduction

NETWORKING

This chapter discusses global principles of communication tuning with a focus on TCP, UDP, and IP protocols.

This chapter is the second part of a series providing detailed steps on diagnosing and improving your AIX TCP/UDP/IP network performance on RISC System/6000s. This chapter discusses global principles of communication tuning with a focus on TCP, UDP, and IP protocols.

This chapter is the last of a three-part series providing detailed steps on improving your AIX TCP/UDP/IP network performance on RISC System/6000s. This chapter discusses global principles of communication tuning with a focus on TCP, UDP, and IP protocols.

What are the various means of connecting PCs to IBM RS/6000 servers running AIX 3.2.5 and 4.1? This chapter answers the question by addressing such topics as terminal emulation; using TCP/IP stacks; file/print sharing; integrating AIX with

NetWare; E-mail; and the impact of Windows 95, Windows NT, and OS/2 Warp on AIX connectivity. In addition, the chapter takes a look at the Distributed Computing Environment, its Distributed File System, and Transarc's AFS.

DATA STORAGE AND MANAGEMENT

details performance characteristics that the UK's National Centre of Competence observed during technical evaluation, and answers some common questions regarding the Accelerator.

This chapter presents an overview of the quorum feature of the AIX Logical Volume Manager (LVM) and discusses the pros and cons of disabling quorum in HACMP/6000 cluster environments. This information should help system administrators make better informed decisions about quorum issues appropriate for their production environments. The chapter assumes that users understand the AIX Logical Volume Manager and HACMP/6000 concepts and terminology.

TECHNOLOGY TRENDS

Lotus Notes is the industry's leading integrated messaging-based client/server groupware solution. After providing a brief overview of Lotus Notes and some of its new Release 4 features, this chapter discusses why AIX Notes servers may make sense in an environment where increased server capacity is needed or improved administration and management are desired. After listing the software and hardware prerequisites, this chapter provides tips for getting started with Lotus Notes for AIX.

This chapter presents direct measurements demonstrating that when the overall ATM environment is properly configured, the TURBOWAYS 100 and 155 ATM adapters can perform close to their designed limits. While the media speed may be 100 or 155 Mbps, several factors — especially workstation configuration and protocol overhead (TCP/IP and ATM) — determine actual throughput of user data.

This technical brief discusses some of the key issues surrounding two emerging interconnection technologies, Fibre Channel and Asynchronous Transfer Mode. The intent is to provide an overview of each standard and examine the relationship between the two.

Rather than describing the PowerPC architecture
in detail, this chapter puts 64-bit technology in
perspective for business and technical people alike.
The chapter reviews the main characteristics of
POWER and PowerPC, introduces and describes
64-bit technology, and lists its advantages. The
chapter discusses the 64-bit implementations of
PowerPC, especially their characteristic aspects,
in addition to the support for 64-bit execution.
Finally, the chapter describes how AIX is likely to
evolve from the current 32-bit support to the new
technology, then summarizes the topics discussed.

This chapter provides a general overview of the four
alternative technologies for delivering highly scalable
computing systems. These technologies — designed
to meet users' growing demands for increased processing power — include large uniprocessors, client/server,
symmetric multi-processors, and parallel systems. The
chapter also highlights IBM development efforts in
each of these areas.

Acknowledgements

This book, indeed the entire series of three volumes, could not have been published without the contributions of a great many people. Particular thanks go to the many technicians, support specialists, programmers, developers, and other AIX professionals who wrote chapters in their area of expertise. Also, the support of Beverly Montgomery, publications manager in IBM's Personal Systems Competency Center, has been vital to the continued success of */AIXtra* magazine.

Special thanks go to the members of the team behind */AIXtra* including Melissa Cox, Donna Su, Terry Pinkston, Bill Carr, Dollie Hunley, Ruth Smith, and Dave Willburn. One of the most important contributions to this volume in the series came from Tammy Alana, who was responsible for the final coordination of the manuscript.

On a personal note, I have to thank the finest journalism teachers anyone could ever have, E.J. and Nancy Hodel, my parents, and my wife, Dianne Hodel, the mother of our two sons, Grant and Kirk.

Thanks to you all.

Alan E. Hodel

Alan E. Hodel
Dallas, Texas
Summer 1996

An Introduction

On February 15, 1990, IBM introduced the RISC System/6000* family, a series of nine high-performance workstations and servers that offered, at the time, leading-edge technology and power. The new systems were based on two key pillars of technology — one hardware, one software. These technologies ultimately enabled IBM to emerge from relative obscurity as an also-ran in the UNIX marketplace and take its place among the leaders in UNIX-based systems.

The two key technologies behind the February 1990 product announcement were IBM's new Performance Optimization With Enhanced RISC (POWER) Architecture* — the RS/6000's central processing unit (CPU), or microprocessor — and AIX*, IBM's implementation of the popular UNIX operating system (OS). POWER Architecture was an advanced, second-generation superscalar implementation of Reduced Instruction Set Computing (RISC) technology. (Although IBM researchers invented RISC technology some years earlier, the company never fully exploited the technology until the RS/6000* family arrived in 1990.)

While other versions of the AIX OS had been available on other platforms prior to the RISC System/6000's launch, their market presence was relatively small when compared with other vendors in the UNIX market. The new version of the AIX OS, tailored to the RS/6000 family, demonstrated IBM's commitment to the UNIX-based open systems environment.

IBM's AIX operating system, which has been upgraded several times since the original introduction (the latest variant available as of this writing is AIX Version 4.2), was based on UNIX System V and 4.3 BSD and conformed to the Portable Operating Systems for Computer Environments (POSIX*) IEEE* Standard 1003.1-1988. Upwardly compatible with AT&T's UNIX System V, AIX Version 3 included extensions from UNIX V.2 and V.3 required to conform to SVID Issue 2. Follow-on releases of AIX were designed to comply with XPG3 and, later, with XPG4.

The AIX operating system includes a variety of features that are distinct improvements over earlier UNIX implementations, such as physical disk space management, an advanced file system, program management facilities, extended realtime support, and enhanced virtual memory. The OS provides improved system management and network install facilities like X.25, Transmission Control Protocol/Internet Protocol (TCP/IP), and Network File Server (NFS*).

Once the RISC System/6000 family became available in mid-1990, IBM began development of a support effort designed to assist AIX users. That effort included the launch, in 1991, of a technical magazine devoted to coverage of AIX- and POWER-related topics and associated products from IBM and other vendors. Originally a quarterly publication, */AIXtra: IBM's Magazine For AIX Professionals* has grown from a circulation of less than 4,300 to nearly 45,000 and is now published bimonthly. This anthology is the third volume of some of the most popular technical articles from */AIXtra* magazine.

Alan E. Hodel

Alan E. Hodel
Editor
hodel@vnet.ibm.com

*Alan E.Hodel has edited and produced regional, national, and international business publications in both print and online versions. He has served as publisher and editor of */AIXtra: IBM's Magazine For AIX Professionals *since founding it in 1991. Hodel, who has been with IBM 11 years, also is editor in chief of *SQ: IBM's Magazine of Software Technologies, *which debuted in 1994. He serves on the Advisory Board for UNIX Expo, is a member of the Society for Technical Communication and the American Society of Business Press Editors, and has a bachelor's in journalism from West Virginia University.*

Networking

TCP/IP and SNA:
A Business Partnership Whose Time Has Come

10 Steps to Improve
AIX TCP/IP Network Performance – Part 1

10 Steps to Improve
AIX TCP/IP Network Performance – Part 2

10 Steps to Improve
AIX TCP/IP Network Performance – Part 3

PC-to-AIX Connectivity: RISCs and Rewards

Reid Sayre

Reid Sayre is a senior programmer with IBM, currently working in product development for the AIX SNA product family. Sayre has been with IBM for 26 years with various responsibilities in both host and PC architecture, design, development, and testing before moving to the AIX SNA development platform in 1992.

TCP/IP and SNA: A Business Partnership Whose Time Has Come

By Reid Sayre

TCP/IP and SNA are major players in today's multiprotocol networking environment. This chapter describes how a manufacturing company used IBM solutions to resolve interconnectivity issues — issues the parent company faced after it acquired two smaller businesses. The parent company needed to integrate TCP/IP and SNA networks, expand into open systems, and update its manufacturing processes. SNA Server for AIX, SNA Client Access for AIX, and SNA Application Access for AIX are the core products described in this chapter.

It's a safe bet that Transmission Control Protocol/Internet Protocol (TCP/IP) is the most commonly used networking protocol in the UNIX world. The other side of the coin, however, is the incredible volume of critical business data still residing on mainframes. More often than not, these critical data are not directly accessible through TCP/IP.

Why not? Because many large enterprises have deployed IBM Systems Network Architecture (SNA) networks as their mainstay protocol. They deploy SNA because it offers the industrial-strength security, accuracy, speed, and integrity vital to industrial-strength manufacturing, finance, banking, and retail operations. Alternately, users of other networking technologies such as TCP/IP also need access to the centralized host system data; therefore, some sort of gateway is required.

Savvy businesspeople increasingly appreciate the value of distributed UNIX systems — and particularly IBM's AIX flavor. According to an International Data Corporation report, the UNIX market as a whole grew about 20 percent in 1994; the AIX market doubled that. These same businesspeople also value the security that legacy architectures offer. Since AIX allows TCP/IP and SNA traffic to merge easily on the same network, businesses can now securely distribute their valuable legacy data.

A Typical Scenario

To illustrate how these issues of open systems, security, interconnectivity, and productivity play out, this chapter describes a manufacturing company that expands its product line by acquiring two smaller businesses to leverage its strengths. To exploit this competitive advantage, the parent company must update its data communications network as well as its manufacturing processes.

Top management in the parent company requires that the new system have the following capabilities:

◆ The newly acquired businesses, primarily TCP/IP-based, must be able to access central host data.

◆ The new businesses' many applications (which will reside on AIX systems) must be accessible by users who currently run 3270-type displays.

◆ There must be one primary network, to contain costs and to deliver data quickly, accurately, and securely.

◆ The current manufacturing processes must become more automated.

◆ Materials must be tracked through the manufacturing process.

The Solutions

While the overall plan requires coordination, the company can implement the new network in several discrete stages:

◆ Connecting AIX systems to an existing SNA network

◆ Connecting a TCP/IP network to an SNA network with an AIX system gateway

◆ Accessing new AIX applications from the existing SNA network

◆ Running TCP/IP sockets applications over an SNA network

Connecting AIX Systems to an Existing SNA Network

Small, customized AIX systems out on the manufacturing floor will perform vital manufacturing management functions for:

◆ Gathering data — as parts move through the manufacturing process

◆ Reading bar codes — from work orders printed from various sites on the shop floor

◆ Controlling machine tools — from new customized applications that the new engineering staffs write

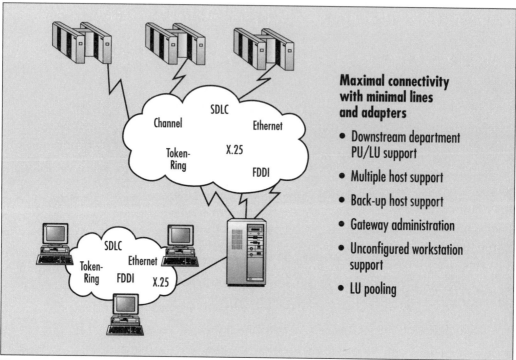

Maximal connectivity
with minimal lines
and adapters

- Downstream department PU/LU support

- Multiple host support

- Back-up host support

- Gateway administration

- Unconfigured workstation support

- LU pooling

Figure 1. SNA Server for AIX Gateway Capabilities

◆ Connecting the manufacturing floor and central database — by serving as gateways and concentrators

◆ Emulating 3270-type terminals — so that personnel on the manufacturing floor can access the central inventory database

◆ Distributing function — among the central database, gateways, and endpoint manufacturing stations

Figure 1 illustrates this part of the overall configuration. Each endpoint manufacturing station contains either an SNA Server for AIX and custom Advanced Program-to-Program Communications (APPC) applications for accessing the host database or 3270-emulator programs for interactively accessing existing host applications. Connecting the endpoint boxes to the mainframes is an SNA Server for AIX configured as an SNA gateway to concentrate the 3270 traffic.

One significant aspect of the Figure 1 configuration is how the SNA Server for AIX can connect to any of the following:

◆ Synchronous Data Link Control (SDLC)

◆ Token-Ring

◆ Ethernet

◆ Fiber Distributed Data Interface (FDDI)

◆ X.25

◆ IBM System/390 channel, block multiplexor, or ESCON

In addition, SNA Server for AIX includes the following features:

◆ An emulator interface (for example, IBM 3270 host connection program for communicating with 3270 applications)

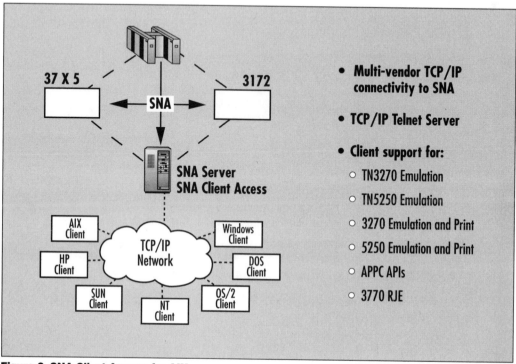

Figure 2. SNA Client Access for AIX

◆ The Common Programming Interface for Communications (CPI-C) and a lower level APPC interface for communicating with other APPC and CPI-C applications. (**Note:** The APPC and CPI-C programming interfaces allow users to write their own programs that use these APIs to communicate with other APPC and CPI-C implementations such as DB2 and CICS. In addition, some applications such as DB2 have their own distributed client function that uses APPC and CPI-C to communicate with matching server function.)

◆ An implementation of APPN, including Network Node (NN), End Node (EDN), and Low Entry Networking (LEN)

◆ The entire APPC Application Suite, including

   ◇ File transfer

   ◇ Connectivity testing

   ◇ Simple messaging

   ◇ Remote command execution

   ◇ Name server

◆ Tools to help develop APPC and CPI-C applications

◆ Complete softcopy documentation including an advanced hypertext browser

Connecting a TCP/IP Network to an SNA Network with an AIX System Gateway

To continue the scenario, assume that one of the businesses the parent company acquires is an engineering and design shop with an internal TCP/IP network. Now that its engineers and designers have become part of the larger company, they need access to data on the corporate database.

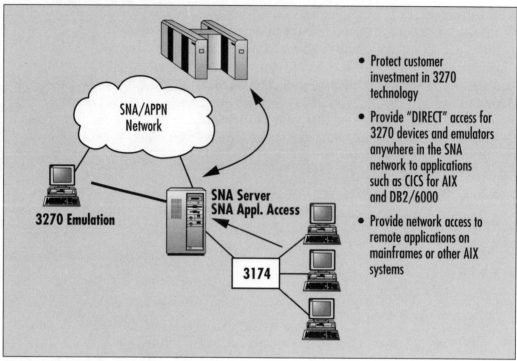

Figure 3. SNA Application Access for AIX

SNA Client Access for AIX, combined with SNA Server for AIX, connects the new shop's TCP/IP network to the existing corporate SNA network (see Figure 2). The Client Access product supplies the TCP/IP connectivity, while the SNA Server for AIX product supplies all of the SNA connectivity.

This approach supports many client products, both IBM and non-IBM. For example, any standard TN3270 or TN5250 client in the TCP/IP part of the network can access unmodified 3270 or 5250 applications in the SNA part. (The TN3270 and TN5250 are standard, publicly documented TCP/IP-to-SNA protocols for interoperability.)

In addition, CNT/Brixton* clients running in various non-IBM UNIX systems can enable remote job entry (RJE) access to the SNA network and can also enable APPC and CPI-C applications not only to operate in the TCP/IP part of the network, but also to access APPC and CPI-C applications in the SNA part of the network. (**Note**: The IBM SNA Client Access for AIX and the IBM SNA Application Access for AIX products resulted from a 1994 agreement between IBM and CNT/Brixton. CNT/Brixton has implemented a set of standard APPC-to-TCP/IP protocols for RJE and CPI-C/APPC.)

To protect the overall system, security features in the IBM SNA Client Access for AIX product restrict specific IP addresses from accessing specific hosts.

Accessing New AIX Applications
From the Existing SNA Network

For the parent company to expand its manufacturing enterprise, it must develop new applications on AIX systems. While all users may eventually move to distributed systems, it would not be cost effective to move everyone immediately. Terminal users today, therefore, must be able to access the new AIX applications from classical 3270 terminals. SNA Applications Access for AIX provides this function, as Figure 3 illustrates.

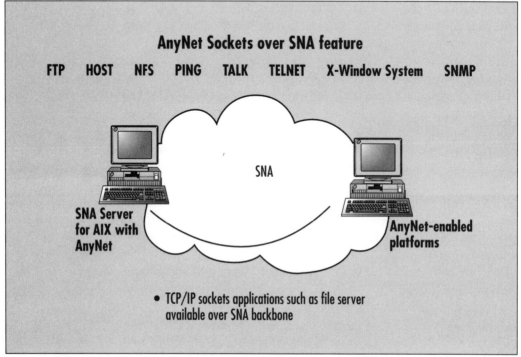

Figure 4. SNA Server's AnyNet Sockets over SNA Feature

Although every company may not need every available feature, Figure 3 illustrates how SNA terminals can access AIX applications through either of the following paths:

◆ SNA Application Access for AIX can own and control the SNA terminals. In this case, Application Access supplies the logon prompts and initial application routing. A terminal owned by Application Access can log on to either a local AIX application such as CICS for AIX or can log on to an application such as CICS/ESA residing elsewhere in the network.

◆ A terminal owned elsewhere in the network (such as VTAM) can access an AIX application such as CICS for AIX. The terminal can be directly host-attached or can reside anywhere in the SNA network, even across SNA network boundaries.

Either way, whether the 3270 terminals are host-controlled or not, they can access AIX applications. Users have a choice in how they set up their networks.

Running TCP/IP Sockets Applications over an SNA Network

Suppose that the second engineering and design shop acquired has its own set of design applications written to the sockets interface. Within the newly integrated company, both design shops would find these applications useful and, once the shops are connected, could share application data. Typically, sockets applications operate over TCP/IP networks, but the parent company chooses not to pay the cost of duplicating networks.

How do they get around this problem? SNA Server's AnyNet "sockets over SNA" function solves it. As diagrammed in Figure 4, once the systems are connected with SNA, sockets applications can run over the SNA network. In addition to customer written sockets applications, the following standard applications run in this environment:

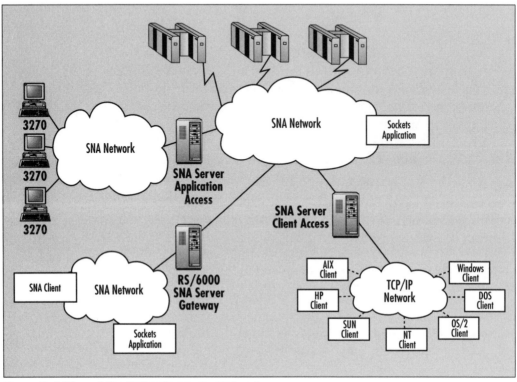

Figure 5. A View of the Entire Corporate Network

◆ FTP (file transfer protocol)

◆ NFS (network file system)

◆ PING (packet internet groper)

◆ TALK (a command allowing two users on the same or different hosts to have an interactive conversation)

◆ TELNET (the U.S. Department of Defense's virtual terminal protocol, based on TCP/IP)

◆ SNMP (simple network management protocol)

◆ X-Windows (a UNIX-based window system called "X"; a specification for device-independent windowing operations on bitmap display devices)

Some sockets applications, especially those that send large blocks of data — ftp, for example — actually run faster than they do over native TCP/IP. It is significant that the AnyNet functions of the IBM SNA Server interoperate with AnyNet functions in other products. AnyNet product functions implement the published multiprotocol transport networking (MPTN) architecture, which is a part of the IBM Open Blueprint.

Since AnyNet has been architected as a general service, these and many other sockets applications can run over the SNA network to systems other than AIX, as Figure 4 illustrates.

Summary

While every situation is different, the above scenario describes how one company has used three IBM products on the AIX platform to deploy state-of-the-art networking technology. Figure 5 shows how all of the pieces fit together in a corporate network.

What is SNA?

SNA is

- IBM's Systems Network Architecture — the descriptions of the logical structure, formats, protocols, and operational sequences for transmitting information units through, and controlling the configuration of, networks.

- A high level networking protocol standard that corresponds to the OSI (Open Systems Interconnect) seven-layer reference model, which was designed to represent how networks transmit data.

- A cost-effective, connection-oriented protocol (*Connection-oriented protocols* transport data in steady streams of packets with predetermined routes. Setting up the routes beforehand helps eliminate congestion and better utilizes network resources. Examples include X.25 and Internet TCP. On the other hand, *connectionless protocols*, also known as datagram services, break each frame of data into one or more separate packets. Examples include LANs and Internet IP.)

- Highly reliable and secure

- Extensively used in wide area networks (WANs)

- Popular in most industries, especially manufacturing, banking, finance, and retail

What is TCP/IP?

TCP is

- Transmission Control Protocol, the transport layer protocol of the TCP/IP networking protocol suite

- The most common protocol on Ethernet and the Internet

- Multi-plexing (combining several independent transmission signals on one communications channel)

- Connection- and stream-oriented

- Reliable

- Capable of providing full-duplex process-to-process connectivity

IP is

- Internet Protocol, the network layer of the TCP/IP networking protocol suite

- Connectionless (or a "best-attempt" method for transmitting data packets over several routes in varying speeds and not necessarily in their original order. The destination node may then need to put them in order.)

This chapter has covered several interactions and combinations of SNA and multiprotocol networking. Many more are possible and may be described in future chapters.

Product and Technical Support Information
Following are the program numbers you can use to order the products.

◆ AIX SNA Server for AIX (program number 5765-582)

◆ SNA Client Access for AIX (program number 5696-944)

◆ SNA Application Access for AIX (program number 5696-943)

For more detailed information about these products and IBM support offerings, contact the following sources:

◆ Product Information Line: (919) 254-9192

◆ FAX Response Line: (919) 254-7349

◆ E-mail: `snaserv@vnet.ibm.com`

◆ IBM's AIX Support Family: (800) CALL-AIX (225-5249); FAX: (817) 962-6723; E-mail: `callaix@vnet.ibm.com`

◆ IBM's AIX SNA Networking Family Home Page: `http://www.raleigh.ibm.com/asf/asfprod.html`

◆ IBM's Networking Services and Support Home Page: `http://www.raleigh.ibm.com/netres.html`

Sam Nokes
IBM Corporation
11400 Burnet Road
Austin, TX 78758
snokes@vnet.ibm.com

As a member of IBM's National
Technical Support Organization,
the AIX Systems Center, Mr. Nokes
provides AIX Communication and
Network Performance support. He
has more than six years of UNIX
communications programming and
support experience.

10 Steps to Improve AIX TCP/IP Network Performance – Part 1

By Sam Nokes

This chapter is the first of a series providing detailed steps on diagnosing and improving your AIX TCP/UDP/IP network performance on RISC System/6000s. This chapter discusses global principles of communication tuning with a focus on TCP, UDP, and IP protocols.

Knowing something is wrong and recognizing the problem are the most important steps in network performance monitoring and tuning. Add eight more and you've got the following step-by-step guide for monitoring and tuning AIX Transmission Control Protocol/Internet Protocol (TCP/IP) performance on the RISC System/6000.

The 10 steps include:
1. Establish a starting point
2. Understand the problem
3. Devise a plan
4. Look for signs of trouble
5. Select the right tool for the job
6. Monitor and collect performance data
7. Analyze your performance data
8. Handle performance problems
9. Tune your network environment
10. Review changes

Part one of this series covers the first four steps — from determining where the problem is to looking for signs of trouble. The following installments will describe the last six steps — from selecting the right tool for the job to reviewing the changes made during the previous nine steps. So, if your AIX TCP/UDP/IP network could use a tune up, read on to find out just how to do it.

Step 1: "Is It Me or the Network?" — Establish a Starting Point
A few months ago, I was greeted by a customer who explained his telnet sessions were "incredibly slow...taking what seemed like 10 seconds to display a character when he was the only one on the system — at midnight!" He attributed the behavior to a slow server, though a number of other network factors could have been the root of the problem. Actually, the problem was on another system, which was flooding the network with broadcasts by issuing the

rwho command from a `cron` job. It had nothing at all to do with his
system or his server system.

The point is this, network performance trouble-shooting, monitoring, and tuning is not exactly straightforward. Even in the simplest
case of a two-node network, many hardware and software parameters
exist whose interdependencies can impact network performance
significantly. Typically, the approach to such complex problems begins
with breaking the sum into pieces, then proceeds to establishing a
starting point and executing a systematic and logical plan of attack,
eliminating the possible causes until a solution is reached.

So where do you start? A skilled network analyst always starts
with a complete understanding of the current network environment.
Generally, this approach implies documentation of the network
topology, applications, and protocols. If the network configuration
is unknown, use the `ping -R hostname` and/or the `traceroute`
commands to chart the network paths a datagram will take.

The `ping -R` option enables the IP record route feature, which
causes every router that handles the datagram to add its IP address to
a list in the IP options field. The maximum size of an IP header limits
the usefulness of the record route (RR) option. Most routes contain
more hops than the 40 option bytes can represent. Recall the IP header
length is limited to 60 bytes. Thus, you can calculate the maximum
hops as follows: 60 bytes – 20 byte fixed header – 3 byte RR overhead
= 37 bytes/4 byte IP address length = 9 IP addresses.

The `traceroute` command, available with PTF U491190 and
AIX 3.2.5, likewise outputs the route that IP packets take to a
network host but accumulates the information a little differently.
The `traceroute` command uses two techniques, small `ttl` (time
to live) values and an invalid port number, to trace packets to their
destination. `traceroute` sends out a user datagram protocol (UDP)
packet with small `ttl` values to detect the intermediate gateways.

The ttl values start at one and increase in increments of one for each group of three UDP packets traceroute sends. When a gateway receives a packet, it decrements the ttl.

If the ttl is then zero, the intervening system does not forward the packet and returns an Internet control message protocol (ICMP) time exceeded message to the source of the packet [1]. The key to traceroute is that the IP datagram containing the ICMP time exceeded message has the router's (incoming) IP address as the source address.

> !!Warning!! The traceroute command was created for use in network testing, measurement, and management. You should use it primarily for manual fault isolation. Because of the load it imposes on the network, you should not use the traceroute command during normal operations or from automated scripts.

To complete your documentation, include a network baseline, which details what your network looks like when it's running well. Users often report performance problems right after some change to the system's hardware or software is made. Unless the documentation contains a pre-change baseline measurement with which to compare post-change performance, problem quantification is impossible.

To create a full set of performance and configuration information, use the PerfPMR package. On AIX Version 3.2.5, PerfPMR is an informal tool available from your IBM representative. On AIX Version 4.1, PerfPMR is an optional package you can install from the AIX base operating system distribution medium.

To get the most complete data possible, you should run perfpmr 3600 during the busiest hour of the day. The output files from this measurement run will appear in the directory /var/perf/tmp. (If you are running on a pre-Version 4 system, the output files will appear in the current working directory.) Be sure to move these files to a safe haven for future reference. If possible, establish what's "normal" by monitoring the traffic for a few months.

Step 2: "Get a Bead on Your Target" — Understand the Problem
In a nutshell, the following factors limit AIX TCP/IP performance:

◆ The relative speed of the underlying hardware media

◆ The pathlengths or CPU cycles needed to execute a given piece of code

◆ The size of the packets of data being transferred

◆ The efficiency with which the data are cached in the memory on the client, intermediate, and server systems

◆ The quality of the users' code that accesses the LAN subsystem

Thus, to understand the problem, you need to understand how each of these factors contributes to poor network performance.

All stations attached to the LAN share media bandwidth. Consequently, the more stations that are attempting to transmit data, the smaller the share of bandwidth for each station. Given that the Ethernet bandwidth limit today is usually 10 Mbps and token-rings currently run at 4 Mbps or 16 Mbps, it is quite possible that, with powerful servers and hundreds of clients, LANs can almost saturate the physical media providing interconnection. This saturation is much more likely to occur in Ethernet networks due to the broadcast/collision detection/re-broadcast nature of that architecture. Step 8: Handling Performance Problems discusses some ways to ease this problem.

Next, consider an end-host CPU, which is loaded with work and has only a few free CPU cycles. Here, the time it takes to execute a given piece of network related code could impact TCP/UDP/IP performance considerably. As a system runs out of memory and begins paging local applications, the page fault handling consumes the CPU rather than network requests. System performance tuning may be the answer; however, this subject is beyond the scope of this chapter. The */AlXtra* September/October 1993 article on `vmstat` by Russ Heise and the January/February 1994 article on `iostat` by Barry Saad both cover this subject well and are recommended reading.

The size of a data packet also plays a role in limiting network performance. Conventional wisdom says that bigger packets are better because sending fewer big packets "costs less" than sending more smaller packets. This reasoning assumes the packets are not large enough to cause fragmentation, since fragmentation introduces another set of problems. The reduced cost is that associated with the network (packet header overhead), routers (routing decisions), and hosts (protocol processing and device interrupts). Step 7 provides more information about packet (i.e., maximum transmission unit [MTU]) sizing.

A burst of frames can also exceed a node's ability to receive if that server does not have the memory resources to queue the incoming packets in a protocol-specific structure. As a result, the receiving node will drop some frames. If congestion in the receiving system continues, the network can eventually become unstable.

Consider this example. Station A sends a request to a network server. When the server receives the request, it sends a stream of frames back to the source node. However, due to the congestion in the intermediate systems or source node, frames are discarded. After the initial timeout interval expires, the source node will resend the request to the server, and the server will retransmit all frames back to the source node. Again, the source node or intermediate system does not have the ability to receive all frames due to the congestion or deficiencies in memory caching, so some frames are discarded. This behavior is often called the "ping-pong" phenomenon.[2] Steps 6 through 8 provide tips to eliminate this condition.

Finally, network performance can suffer as a result of poorly written code. Whenever possible, AIX communication application programs should read and write in quantities of either less than or equal to 935 bytes, or slightly less than or equal to 4,096 bytes (or multiples thereof). A read or write of less than or equal to 935 bytes will be placed in one to four mbufs; a read or write of less than or equal to 4,096 bytes (or multiples thereof) will make efficient use of the clusters that are used for writes larger than 935 bytes. If you are developing AIX communication applications, a detailed discussion of this topic can be found in Chapter 8 of the *AIX Performance Tuning Guide*.[3]

Step 3: Know Where You're Going — Devise A Plan

As this chapter mentioned at the outset, you should consider a number of logical and physical components when analyzing TCP/UDP/IP performance degradation. Recall in a client/server architecture, client and server systems are constructed from a number of interconnected components. Each component provides an interface through which it communicates with other components. Thus, communication between clients and servers can be viewed as communication between relevant components. The Open System Interconnection (OSI) model logically breaks up the job of moving data from one point to another into seven different components as shown in Figure 1.

Thus, one approach to data communication performance analysis is to follow the OSI communications model.

A brief review of the data flow beginning with data generation at the application layer will help determine the potential bottlenecks that can occur. Consider Figure 2, the TCP/UDP/IP data flow diagram.

Send (Illustrated on the left-hand side of Figure 2)

In the AIX operating system, applications that use TCP/UDP/IP protocols to communicate across networks must use sockets to access those protocols. In the application layer, a program needing access to network communication first opens a socket, specifying the type of socket, which will usually be either TCP or UDP. The semantics of opening, reading, and writing to sockets are similar to those for manipulating files. As an application writes to a socket, the data are copied from the user space into the socket send buffer in kernel space. The socket send buffer is made up of smaller buffers called mbufs, which are organized into linked lists.

An mbuf is a type of kernel buffer that uses pinned system memory for storage and comes in two sizes: a 256 Kbyte mbuf that holds 236 Kbytes of data and an "mbuf cluster" (known simply as a cluster) that holds 4,096 Kbytes of data. The AIX operating system provides a pool of free mbufs and clusters and mbuf management services to various layers for their buffering needs. Depending on the amount of data the application is copying into the socket send buffer, the socket will put the data into mbufs or clusters.

Once the application program copies the data into the socket send buffer, the socket layer calls the TCP layer, passing it a pointer to the linked list of mbufs (mbuf chain). (See "Tuning the mbuf Pools" in the *AIX Performance Guide* for a more comprehensive discussion of the mbuf facility.)

The TCP layer allocates a new mbuf for its header information and copies the data in the socket send buffer either into the TCP header mbuf if there is room or into a newly allocated mbuf chain. If the data being copied are in clusters, the data are not actually copied into new clusters.

Instead, the code sets a pointer field in the new mbuf header (this header is part of the mbuf structure and is unrelated to the TCP header) to point to the cluster(s) containing the data, thereby avoiding the overhead of a four KB copy. TCP then checksums the data, updates its various state variables, which are used for flow control and other services, and finally calls the IP layer with the header mbuf now linked to the new mbuf chain (in the TCP layer, this chain is termed a segment). The maximum size of a segment is based on the maximum transmission unit (MTU) for the interface.

The IP layer determines to what interface the mbuf chain should be sent, updates and checksums the IP part of the header sent from TCP, and passes the chain (a packet to IP) to the IF (interface) layer. The IF layer prepends the link layer header information in the TCP/IP header mbuf, checks the format of the mbufs to make sure they conform to the device driver's input specifications, and then calls the device driver write routine. At the device driver layer, the mbuf chain containing the data is enqued on the transmit queue, and the adapter is signaled to start transmission/Direct Memory Access operations. At this point, control returns up the path to the TCP output routine, which will continue sending as long as it has more data to send. If it does not have more packets to send, control returns to the application, which then runs asynchronously while the adapter is busy transmitting data. When the adapter has completed transmission, it interrupts the system, and the device interrupt routines are called to adjust the transmit queues and free the mbufs that held the transmitted data.

Receive (Illustrated on the righthand side of Figure 2)
On the receive side, an application will open a socket and attempt to read data from it. If there are no data in the socket receive buffer, the socket layer will cause the application to go to the sleep state (blocking) until data arrive. When an adapter receives packets, they are direct memory accessed from the adapter into a driver-managed receive queue. Then, the adapter interrupts the system. The receive

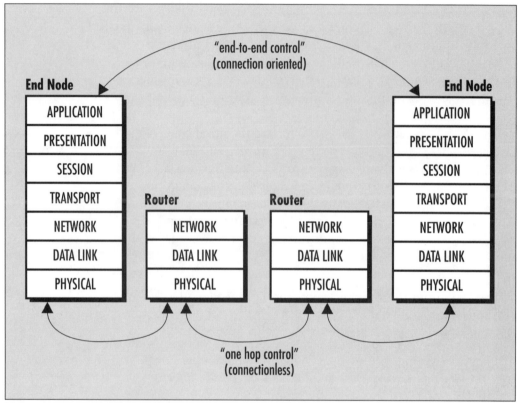

Figure 1. Layers in a Router Network

queue may consist of mbufs, or the device driver may manage a separate pool of buffers for the device; in either case, the data are in an mbuf chain when it is passed from the device driver to the IF layer.

In AIX Version 3, the IF layer removes the link header and enqueues the mbuf chain (done with pointers, not copy) on the IP input queue and schedules an off-level interrupt to do the IP input processing. When the off-level interrupt occurs, the IP input routine dequeues the mbuf chain, checks the IP header checksum to make sure the header was not corrupted, determines if the packet is for this system, and, if so, passes the mbuf chain to the TCP input routine.

In AIX Version 4, the demux layer (equated to the IF layer in Version 3) calls IP on the interrupt thread. No further scheduling or queuing/dequeuing activity exists. IP checks the IP header checksum to make sure the header did not become corrupt and determines if the packet is for this system. If so, and the frame is not a fragment, IP passes the mbuf chain to the TCP or UDP input routine.

The TCP input routine checksums the TCP header and data for corruption detection, determines which connection these data are for, removes its header information, links the mbuf chain onto the socket receive buffer associated with this connection, and uses a socket service to wake up the application if it is sleeping as described earlier. The socket layer copies the data stored in the socket receive buffer into the application's buffer and then frees the mbuf chain. Execution control then passes back to the application.[3]

Based on the above process and the ISO seven-layer model, Figure 3 outlines several parameters that will affect AIX TCP/UDP/IP protocols.

With these parameters in mind, the game plan is to initiate a problem determination approach with progressive elimination of common resource problems, moving from the local RS/6000 system

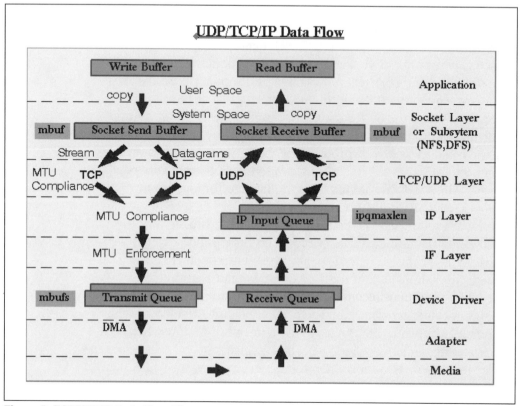

Figure 2. TCP/UDP/IP Data Flow Diagram

out onto the network and then to the remote nodes following the seven-layer OSI model as a reference.

Step 4: Be Alert — Look for Signs of Trouble

When experiencing performance problems, generally, the first thing you should check for is any types of errors. Errors cause many performance problems that, although not fatal, cause timeouts or retransmission of the data as discussed in Step 2.

Errors can occur on different communication layers such as the physical layer (a line of bad quality) or the network layer (errors in the IP header, for example). You can diagnose a large percentage of these problems by simply reviewing the AIX system error log. To view the error log, issue the command `errpt -a|pg`. The `errpt` entries are self-documenting. Most entries in the error log are attributable to hardware and software problems, but the system can also log informational messages. On token-ring networks, it's not uncommon to find entries like that in Figure 4, indicating that a piece of hardware (the token-ring) may become unavailable soon due to numerous errors the device driver reported. Sometimes these failures result from a token-ring adapter becoming unplugged from its MAU, which causes the adapter to suffer a lobe error.

Typically some adapter is misbehaving in some unknown way but stays attached to the network. In this case, the usual response will be for the network to go into a beaconing mode. Beaconing notifies the rest of the ring that an adapter has detected an error as a result of a station not receiving the tokens for a user-specified number of seconds. Therefore, not all errors will initiate beaconing — only those that destroy the signal or produce the effect of an open ring. This process continues until the user clears the error or removes the station that caused the error from the ring.

SUBSYSTEM OR LAYER	NETWORK OPTION PARAMETER
Memory (mbuf) Management	thewall, [lowclust, lowmbuf, and mb_cl_hiwat (AIX Version 3 only)]
Application	At the application layer, the size of the buffer written to the socket is very important in achieving the highest throughput for a particular interface.
Socket Layer	sb_max
TCP/UDP Layer	tcp/udp_sendspace, tcp/udp_recvspace, rfc1323
Internet Protocol (IP) Layer	ipqmaxlen, ipfragttl time
Interface (IF) Layer	MTU
Device Driver	TRANSMIT queue size (xmt_que_size) RECEIVE queue size (rec_que_size) Receive data transfer OFFSET

Figure 3. Comparison of ISO Layers and Affected Network Option Parameters

For Ethernet networks, you should check for ENT_ERR2 entries. The ENT_ERR2 errors are indications of heavy Ethernet loading since packet drops are occurring due to max collisions. Basically, the Ethernet adapter has tried to send a packet and a packet collision occurred, so it stopped for a while before retrying again. If the retry fails 16 times, the system will drop the packet, and the device driver will log the ENT_ERR2 error. Usually the higher layers can recover the packet. However, ENT_ERR2 errors can also be logged if the device driver is not properly designed or configured correctly, or the adapter is malfunctioning.

Reference the "Error class" and "type" fields for additional information. These fields are decoded in Figure 5.

Error log entries also lists probable causes for the error, along with some recommended actions. Finally, the sense data from the adapter are displayed. The sense data are data retrieved directly from the adapter that the device driver used to determine the error. Use the diag program to read and interpret errlog sense data.

For the Fiber Distributed Data Interface (FDDI) adapter, you can interpret the sense data by referring to the "FDDI Error Identifiers for the Error Log" section in InfoExplorer. Other Error Identifier sections of InfoExplorer for other adapters offer varying amounts of useful information.

Besides the system error log, the wise network analyst will also factor network traffic overhead in all data reviews. For example:

◆ Overhead in the protocols (such as headers and trailers in packets), which usually cannot be changed

◆ Exchange of topology data between routers, which certain parameters can influence to some extent such as frequency of data exchange and keep-alive messages

```
ERROR LABEL:       TOK_BEACON2
ERROR ID:          AEC7B1B0

Date/Time:         Fri Jun 23 14:26:57
Sequence Number:   112811
Machine Id:        000368243100
Node Id:           host1
Error Class:       H
Error Type:        PERM
Resource Name:     tok0
Resource Class:    adapter
Resource Type:     tokenring
Location:          00-02
VPD:
    Network Address  . . . . . . . . . . . . . . . . . . . . . . . . .10005AA83934
    Displayable Message  . . . . . . . . . . . . . . . . . . . . . . .TOKEN RING
    EC Level . . . . . . . . . . . . . . . . . . . . . . . . . . . . . . .C24551
    FRU Number . . . . . . . . . . . . . . . . . . . . . . . . . . . . .022F9380
    Manufacturer . . . . . . . . . . . . . . . . . . . . . . . . . . .VEN0CLT96G
    Part Number  . . . . . . . . . . . . . . . . . . . . . . . . . . . .074F8653
    Serial Number  . . . . . . . . . . . . . . . . . . . . . . . . . . . .014944
    ROS Level and ID . . . . . . . . . . . . . . . . . . . . . . . . . . . .0000
    Loadable Microcode Level . . . . . . . . . . . . . . . . . . . . . . . . .00

Error Description
TOKEN-RING INOPERATIVE

Probable Causes
TOKEN-RING FAULT DOMAIN

Failure Causes
TOKEN-RING FAULT DOMAIN

    Recommended Actions
    REVIEW LINK CONFIGURATION DETAIL DATA
    CONTACT TOKEN-RING ADMINISTRATOR RESPONSIBLE FOR THIS LAN
    REQUEST VERIFICATION OF MANAGEMENT SERVER REPORTING LINKS

Detail Data
SENSE DATA
0ACA 0032 A440 0001 0000 0000 0000 0000 0000 0000 0000 0000 0000 0000 40A0 0000
0000 0010 0000 0000 0000 0000 0000 0000 0000 0000 0000 0000 78CC 0000 0000 0001
C88F 0206 E4EF 0000 1000 5AA8 3934 1000 5AA8 3934 3030 3030 0000 0000 0000 0000
0000 0000 0000 0000 0000 0000 0000 0000 0000 0000 0000 0000 0000 0000 0000 0000
0000 0000 0000 0000 0000 0000 0000 0000 0000 0000 0000 0000 0000 0000 0000 0000
0000 0000 0000 0000
ADDITIONAL SUBVECTORS
0000 0000 0000 0000 0000 0000
---------------------------------------------------------------------------------
```

Figure 4. Examples of `errrpt` **Entries**

```
ERROR LABEL:      ENT_ERR2
ERROR ID:         ABB81CD5

Date/Time:        Thu Aug 4 14:15:26
Sequence Number:  51100
Machine Id:       000049177000
Node Id:          host2
Error Class:      H
Resource Name:    ent0
Resource Class:   adapter
Resource Type:    ethernet
Location:         00-02

VPD:
    Network Address  . . . . . . . . . . . . . . . . . . . . . .02608C2CA290
    ROS Level and ID . . . . . . . . . . . . . . . . . . . . . . . . .0015
    Displayable Message  . . . . . . . . . . . . . . . . . .802.3/ETHERNET
    Part Number  . . . . . . . . . . . . . . . . . . . . . . . . .000G3369
    EC Level . . . . . . . . . . . . . . . . . . . . . . . . . . . .C73859
    Device Driver Level  . . . . . . . . . . . . . . . . . . . . . . . .01
    Diagnostic Level . . . . . . . . . . . . . . . . . . . . . . . . . .01
    FRU Number . . . . . . . . . . . . . . . . . . . . . . . . . .000G3368
    Serial Number  . . . . . . . . . . . . . . . . . . . . . . . .00102556
    Manufacturer . . . . . . . . . . . . . . . . . . . . . . . . . .204491

Error Description
COMMUNICATION PROTOCOL ERROR

Probable Causes
CSMA/CD ADAPTER
CSMA/CD LAN CABLES
LOCAL CSMA/CD ADAPTER CABLE
CABLE TERMINATOR

Failure Causes
LOCAL CSMA/CD ADAPTER
REMOTE CSMA/CD ADAPTER
CSMA/CD LAN CABLES
LOCAL CSMA/CD ADAPTER CABLE

Recommended Actions
PERFORM PROBLEM DETERMINATION PROCEDURES
CHECK CABLE AND ITS CONNECTIONS

Detail Data
SENSE DATA
0000 0082 0600 F58E C115 91CC 0000 0260 8C2C A290 0260 8C2C A290 3030
3135 0004 000F 0000 0000 0000 0000 0009 0000 0001 000C 000E
------------------------------------------------------------------------
```

CLASS	TYPE	DESCRIPTION
H	TEMP	Device may soon become unavailable
H	PERM	Device is unavailable
S	PERM	Software detected fatal error
S	TEMP	Software retries eventually recovered from error

Figure 5. ENT_ERR2 **Log Classifications**

◆ The cost of running tools, which is often proportional to some of the workload (Some performance tools can add significantly to system workload.)

◆ Network management data, including the monitoring of network components

These are the first four steps to improve AIX TCP/IP performance. The following chapters will cover the remaining six steps. The AIX System Center's Consulting and Services team is available for your performance support needs. Contact your local IBM branch office representative, or call the AIX Systems Center at (800) 547-1283 for additonal information, or send an E-mail to `aixserve@dalvm41b.vnet.ibm.com`.

References

[1] Hunt, Craig. *TCP/IP Network Administration*, ISBN 0-937175-82-X, O'Reilly and Associates, Inc., September 1993.

[2] IBM Corp. *Introduction to Performance in Router Networks*, 1st Edition, IBM Publication GG24-4223-00, International Technical Support Organization, 1993.

[3] IBM Corp. AIX Performance Tuning Guide, 4th Edition, IBM Publication SC23-2365-03, 1994.

Sam Nokes
IBM Corporation
11400 Burnet Road
Austin, TX 78758
snokes@vnet.ibm.com

As a member of IBM's National
Technical Support Organization,
the AIX Systems Center, Mr. Nokes
provides AIX Communication and
Network Performance support. He
has more than six years of UNIX
communications programming and
support experience.

10 Steps to Improve AIX TCP/IP Network Performance – Part 2

By Sam Nokes

This chapter is the second part of a series providing detailed steps on diagnosing and improving your AIX TCP/UDP/IP network performance on RISC System/6000s. This chapter discusses global principles of communication tuning with a focus on TCP, UDP, and IP protocols.

Part one discussed how to establish a starting point for problem determination in a network, how to get a good understanding of the problem, how to devise an action plan, and how to look for signs of trouble in the network. Part two will take you through the next two steps: selecting the right tool for the job and monitoring and collecting performance data. The last chapter of this series will provide suggestions for analyzing the performance data, handling performance problems, tuning the network environment, and reviewing network changes.

Step 5: "Choose your Weapon" — Select the Right Tool for the Job

If network analysts are to work smarter, not just harder, to monitor and tune today's distributed, multivendor, multiprotocol networks, they need to have the right tools. Network diagnostic tools, like performance tools for the AIX environment in general, fall into two categories: those that tell you what is going on and those that let you do something about it. Here's a quick overview of some common AIX network performance reporting and analysis tools along with the corresponding Open Systems Interconnection (OSI) layer.

Time Domain Reflectometer (TDR)   Layer 1

For Ethernet networks, probably the most useful tool is a TDR. The TDR attaches to the network in place of one of the terminators. It then puts a signal of known strength and format onto the cable and measures the response. Each type of network fault gives a particular type of reading on the TDR. You must follow the documentation with the device to interpret these readings since the facilities and presentation will vary between devices. It is critical that you correctly set the TDR to measure the parameters of the network — these will vary according to cabling type.

`ifconfig`   Layer 2

You can use the `ifconfig` command to test the physical network interface to determine such information as whether the interface is operational and ready to receive packets, whether you have configured the network interface properly, and the current physical interface Internet address.

`tokstat` (Version 4 only)   Layer 3
The `tokstat` command displays the statistics a specified token-ring device driver gathers. Optionally, you can specify that it display the device-specific statistics in addition to the device driver statistics. You also invoke this command when you run the V4 `netstat` command with the `-v flag`. The `netstat` command, however, does not issue any `tokstat` commands.

`ping`   Layer 3
Packet InterNet Groper (`ping`) sends an echo to a host to determine if the host is accessible. Part of the response you receive from `ping` is the round-trip time. By varying the amount of data and by issuing `ping` to intermediate hosts, you can get an idea of the performance of the underlying networks.

`traceroute`   Layer 3
You can use the `traceroute` command to diagnose Internet connectivity problems by reporting on the current route that packets are taking through the Internet or a network in reaching a specified host.

`iptrace`   Layer 3
You should use `iptrace` whenever you need to look at packets that a machine is sending and receiving, keeping in mind a few things. First, it is a user process that just watches the IP layer on a machine and copies everything that goes through that layer that matches the filters set in the `iptrace` command. As a user process, it must compete with other processes for CPU. Therefore, on a busy machine, `iptrace` may not catch all packets because it loses the CPU and misses them. Also, since `iptrace` sits at the IP layer, you have no

proof that the packet was sent out on the wire, since the packet must pass through the driver and adapter before it gets to the wire. In cases where it is essential to know what is happening on the network, you should use a dedicated network analyzer.

tcpdump (Version 4 only)   Layer 4

The tcpdump command prints out the packet headers the network interface captures that match a boolean expression. If no expression parameter is given, the command will dump all packets on the network.

netstat   Layers 2-4

The netstat command returns a set of statistics concerning the network activity associated with the local host. The netstat command is a good tool to help determine in which area a problem is located. Once you have isolated the problem to an area, you can use more sophisticated tools to proceed. For example, you might use the netstat -i and netstat -v commands to determine if there is a problem with a particular hardware interface and then run the diagnostics to further isolate the problem. Or, if the netstat -s command shows that protocol errors exist, you could then use iptrace for a detailed analysis. Most of the variations of the netstat command use less than 0.2 seconds of CPU time.

netpmon   Layers 2-4

This tool monitors activity and reports statistics on network input/output (I/O) and network-related CPU usage. netpmon will show host traffic at both the device layers and at the TCP and UDP layers. It can also detect traffic to other networks and display network traffic statistics that the host sorts. With a moderate, network-oriented workload, netpmon increases overall CPU utilization by three to five percent. In a CPU-saturated environment with little I/O of any kind, netpmon has slowed a large compile by about 3.5 percent.

Network Analyzers   Layers 2-4

For particular problems, you may have to inspect the contents of data packets on the network using a protocol analyzer. A protocol analyzer captures the complete frame of network data, without regard to the overlying protocols or target network operating system. It treats the frame as raw data. Several commercial packages are available. They will capture data frames and decode them according to the frame type protocol, showing the control information at the relevant layers of the OSI seven-layer model. A protocol analyzer is a very valuable tool but does require some knowledge of network protocols. You also need to be aware that the term "network analyzer" means different things to different vendors. Some vendors may consider a network monitor to be a network analyzer. Monitors record traffic measurements, such as the number of frames transmitted per second or the number of frames that contain errors. These devices are not true analyzers since they are unable to decode the higher-layer protocol information the transmitted frame contains.

IBM SystemView for AIX Performance Reporter   Layers 2-7

Up until now, it has been impossible to get a consolidated view of systems and network performance in a complex and distributed environment. IBM SystemView for AIX Performance Reporter (Performance Reporter) eliminates this problem because it provides effective, informative reports on historical data, generated from its database, which make it easy to follow up service levels with management and customers and to predict problems rather than to react to them. The data collected by Performance Reporter help you identify which users use what resources and analyze bottlenecks and other performance problems. You can gather performance information from AIX, Sun Solaris, and HP-UX nodes. You can easily retrieve data from the Performance Reporter database and use it in other applications. The data model is well documented and easy to modify. Performance Reporter initially supports DB2/6000 and ORACLE.

CRITICAL MEASURES	PerfPMR	netstat -m	ifconfig en0	netstat -in	ipqmaxlen	netstat -s	iptrace tcpdwmp	netstat -v	netpmon	ping -R	ping -s	netstat -I tr0 5
Network loading	✔			✔		✔	✔	✔	✔	✔	✔	✔
Protocols in use	✔			✔		✔	✔	✔	✔	✔	✔	
Frame size dist.	✔			✔		✔	✔		✔	✔	✔	
Busy nodes	✔	✔		✔		✔	✔	✔	✔	✔	✔	✔
Idle nodes	✔	✔		✔		✔	✔	✔	✔	✔	✔	
Unresponsive nodes	✔	✔	✔	✔	✔	✔	✔	✔	✔	✔	✔	
Busiest conversation	✔				✔		✔		✔			
Peak load times & levels	✔				✔		✔		✔			✔
Minimum load times & levels	✔						✔		✔			✔
Node bandwidth usage	✔			✔			✔	✔	✔			✔
Protocol bandwidth usage	✔			✔		✔	✔	✔	✔			✔

Figure 1. A summary of the critical measurements each tool provides when monitoring network performance

BEST/1 for modeling   **Layer 7**

BEST/1 is a capacity-planning tool that uses queuing models to predict the performance of a given configuration when processing a specific workload. You can base the prediction on the workload descriptions from an application design or on workload data acquired by monitoring existing systems. BEST/1 for UNIX is a product of BGS Systems, Inc. BGS Systems can be reached at (617) 891-0000.

Step 6: Monitor and Collect Performance Data

Once you know what network tools will do what jobs, it's time to find out just what's going on with your network. This step is principally concerned with monitoring the activities of Layers 1 through 4 of the OSI seven-layer model. This section takes a commonsense approach to monitoring and collecting relevant performance information, working with the tools presented in Step 5 to perform both protocol analysis and traffic monitoring from the AIX system outward. Figure 1 summarizes the critical measurements each tool provides when monitoring network performance.

The checklist in Figure 1 applies equally well to both network types — Ethernet or token-ring (except where a parameter is specific to one of the transport protocols). The following section discusses the diagnosis you should obtain from the tool. The tools are listed in order, according to the plan described in Step 3.

PerfPMR

Performance Problem Management Report (`PerfPMR`) provides tools and scripts that assist users with data collection for performance problems within AIX systems that may reside in AIX software. The documentation additionally explains:

◆ The responsibilities of problem determination and the role of the Support Centers

```
807 mbufs in use:
      129 mbufs allocated to data
      14 mbufs allocated to packet headers
      190 mbufs allocated to socket structures
      231 mbufs allocated to protocol control blocks
      60 mbufs allocated to routing table entries
      177 mbufs allocated to socket names and addresses
      6 mbufs allocated to interface addresses
      300 mbufs allocated to <mbuf type 42>
   116/339 mapped pages in use
   1557 Kbytes allocated to network (42% in use)
   0 requests for memory denied
   0 requests for memory delayed
   0 calls to protocol drain routines
```

Figure 2. Statistics recorded by the network memory management routines

```
$ ifconfig en0
en0: flags=2000063<UP,BROADCAST,NOTRAILERS,RUNNING,NOECHO>
        inet 9.3.6.14 netmask 0xfffffff0 broadcast 9.3.6.15
```

Figure 3. An example of an `ifconfig` report

◆ The set of criteria for performance and benchmark information (these guidelines can be obtained from a VM disk)

◆ How to recognize valid data and formats of the output

◆ The guidelines for closing a valid Performance PMR

◆ The procedures for PMRs that are not performance problems

U.S. IBM customers can receive the information free of charge from the IBM AIX Support Center. IBM personnel can access the scripts and documentation for AIX 3.2 on a VM tools disk.

Diagnosis: Use the PerfPMR package to obtain a full set of performance and configuration information before you begin. This documentation is essential if further support becomes necessary.

netstat -m

Use netstat -m to get a snapshot of the overall system mbuf usage. Figure 1 shows an example of netstat -m mbuf usage report. The output in the example indicates that 807 small mbufs (256 bytes each) are in use. Also, 116 clusters (4,096 bytes each) are in use, and 1,557 kilobytes (KB) are allocated to the network. To determine the percentage of mbufs used in the example, add 807 mbufs of size 1/4 KB to 116 clusters of size 4 KB, and divide the sum by 1,557 KB allocated to the network, which yields 42 percent. Arithmetically: $(807/4 + 116*4)/1557 = 42/100$.

Diagnosis: See if there are any requests for mbufs denied or delayed. If so, you may need to increase the number of mbufs available to the network. (See Step 7 for mbuf tuning.)

Why?: The mbuf management facility maintains the netstat -m "requests for memory denied" counter and is incremented each time a process cannot satisfy a request for an mbuf allocation. Normally the

$ netstat -in								
NAME	MTU	NETWORK	ADDRESS	Ipkts	Ierrs	Opkts	Oerrs	Coll
lo0	1536	\<Link\>		1083	0	1083	0	0
lo0	1536	127	127.0.0.1	1083	0	1083	0	0
en0	1500	\<Link\>		4286	0	6003	0	0
en0	1500	9.3.6	9.3.6.14	4286	0	6003	0	0
en0	1500	9.3.6.48	9.3.6.52	4286	0	6003	0	0
tr0	1492	\<Link\>		1643208	0	1114853	0	0
tr0	1492	129.35.16	129.35.25.152	1643208	0	1114853	0	0
Note: The collision count for Ethernet is not supported.								

Figure 4. The -in option displays the state of all configured interfaces with the network addresses shown as numbers.

requests for memory denied value will be zero. If a system experiences a high burst of network traffic for which the default configured pools are not sufficient to meet the demand of the incoming burst, the error counter will be incremented once for each mbuf allocation request that fails. Usually in this situation, the counter will number in the thousands due to the large number of packets arriving all at once. The request for memory denied statistic will correspond with dropped packets on the network. Dropped network packets means retransmissions, resulting in degraded network performance.

`ifconfig en0`

The `ifconfig` command configures or displays network interface parameters for a TCP/IP network and indicates unresponsive nodes. Figure 3 shows an example of an `ifconfig` report.

Diagnosis: Determine if the interface is operational and ready to receive packets, if the network interface software is configured properly, and if the Internet address displayed is the correct one currently assigned to the physical interface.

`netstat -in`

`netstat -in` displays statistics about each workstation's network interfaces. The amount of information it displays depends on what command-line options are included. The `-in` option displays the state of all configured interfaces with network addresses shown as numbers (Figure 4).

Diagnosis: Check the maximum transmission unit (MTU) matchup between the server and client. If they are different, make them the same. Also, be aware that if there are slow or wide area networks between the machines, routers, bridges, and other components, you may need to investigate the possibility of fragmentation of the packets that traverse these network segments. Attempt to determine the *smallest* MTU between the source and destination and set the MTU accordingly. (Also see the `netmon` and `ping -R` commands that follow.) Step 7 provides more information on MTUs.

You can ignore the loopback interface, `lo0`, since no network traffic flows through it. `Ierrs` (incoming packet errors) and `Oerrs` (output packet errors) need not be zero, but the value should be very low. Values greater than 100 may indicate a problem such as numerous collisions of the network. Studying the percentage loss and round-trip time statistics that `ping -s` generates may assist in isolating this sort of problem.

If `Oerr` is greater than one percent, the device driver transmit queue is being overrun at the interface-layer. You should increase the transmit queue (`xmt_que_size`) from the System Management Interface Tool (SMIT) devices.

`Ierrs` are much more rare and are often reported for events that do not result in dropped packets. If `Ierrs` are greater than one percent, look at `netstat -m` to see if mbufs are being denied.

Why?: Recall that the interface-layer simply puts on or takes off the header information and passes the remaining packet to the device driver or up to some layer above (IP, DLPI, *etc.*). So `Ierrs` is actually reporting failures in passing the packet up (*i.e.*, to IP).

The only case where AIX will increment `Ierrs` is if it gets a packet type that it is not listening for. That is, if the network is listening for IP packets (includes `tcp`, `arp`, `icmp`, *etc.*) and it receives a packet that is non-IP and passes it up, the packet may fail if there is no upstream listener. Thus, it is debatable whether this situation is really an error. In a sense, it is because AIX received a packet that it ended up dropping, but this error is nothing to really worry about.

Here's a quick reference:

Oerrs > 1% ◆ Transmit queue

◆ Faulty connection

◆ Prolonged periods of collisions

Ierrs > 1% ◆ Bad interface on network

◆ Loose cable

◆ Insufficient buffer space

ipqmaxlen
It is possible, in cases when packets arrive very quickly, for packets to overrun the IP input queue. The AIX operating system provides no simple way to determine if this is happening; however, you can view an overflow counter, using the crash command.[1]

To check this value, start the crash command, and when the prompt appears, type `knlist ipintrq`. This command will return a hexadecimal value to which you should add the value of 10 (hex) and use the sum as an argument for the `od` subcommand. Figure 5 shows an example of the hex value the `crash` command returns.

Diagnosis: If the hex value is greater than 0, overflows have occurred. See Step 7 for resolution.

netstat -s
On occasion, you may want to collect detailed statistics for each protocol on a workstation. Figure 6 shows the kind of output the `netstat -s` tool provides.

By specifying the protocol with the `-p` flag, you can obtain a more concise listing. Figure 6 provides an example of how to use this flag on NFS servers.

```
# crash
> knlist ipintrq
        ipintrq: 0x0149ba68
> od 0149ba78 1
0149ba78: 00000000 <<< This is the value of the IP input queue
                        overflow counter
>quit
```

Figure 5. An example of the `crash` **command hex value**

DIAGNOSIS (with subsets): This tool provides a lot of information. The following diagnosis covers the major points. (Bear in mind, output from a single `netstat` is not as useful as the delta values from two successive `netstat` commands.)

IP: Internet Protocol
The five entries after the total packets received line are all indications of:

◆ Failing hardware in the network

   ◇ Use a network analyzer to investigate further

◆ Failing kernel IP, ICMP, or lower layer protocol software in the network

   ◇ Use `iptrace` to trace where packets are corrupted

   ◇ Use the kernel debug program to debug kernel code

A large number of fragments indicates that protocols above the IP layer on remote hosts are passing data to IP with data sizes larger than the MTU for the interface. Gateways in the network path might also have a much smaller MTU size than the other hosts and gateways.

The cause of dropped packets (*i.e.*, "fragments dropped") could be either multiple paths that packets are taking in the network, causing duplication, or the local host not having enough resources (memory) to handle the volume of incoming traffic.

A large number of fragments dropped after timeout indicates that the network is not fast enough to send all of the IP packet fragments before the time-to-live expires. One solution you can try is increasing the `ipfragttl` network option.

The last three lines of the IP portion of Figure 6 are valuable when the host is functioning as a gateway. A high number of packets that cannot be forwarded indicates that the remote hosts are specifying the local host as a gateway, but the local host does not have the routes to the next hop.

```
ip:
    1312822 total packets received
    0 bad header checksums
    0 with size smaller than minimum
    11 with data size < data length
    0 with header length < data size
    0 with data length < header length
    23589 fragments received
    0 fragments dropped (dup or out of space)
    14 fragments dropped after timeout
    3643 packets forwarded
    60 packets not forwardable
    0 redirects sent
icmp:
    757 calls to icmp_error
    0 errors not generated ĕcuz old message was icmp
    Output histogram:
        echo reply: 1251
        destination unreachable: 674
    0 messages with bad code fields
    0 messages < minimum length
    0 bad checksums
    0 messages with bad length
    Input histogram:
        echo reply: 25
        destination unreachable: 9
        routing redirect: 6
        echo: 1251
    1251 message responses generated
```

Figure 6. `netstat -s` **statistics by protocol, including** `ip,` `icmp,` `tcp,` **and** `udp`

```
tcp:
    1052593 packets sent
        941587 data packets (512301566 bytes)
        353 data packets (361339 bytes) retransmitted
        99692 URG only packets
        0 URG only packets
        4 window probe packets
        7143 window update packets
        3814 control packets
    862314 packets received
        583946 acks (for 512302711 bytes)
        1973 duplicate acks
        0 acks for unsent data
        581198 packets (67078293 bytes) received in-sequence
        150 completely duplicate packets (11176 bytes)
        2 packets with some dup. data (514 bytes duped)
        325 out-of-order packets (11010 bytes)
        6 packets (0 bytes) of data after window
        0 window probes
        3379 window update packets
        94 packets received after close
        0 discarded for bad checksums
        0 discarded for bad header offset fields
        0 discarded because packet too short
    1705 connection requests
    155 connection accepts
    1787 connections established (including accepts)
    1859 connections closed (including 16 drops)
    72 embryonic connections dropped
    524216 segments updated rtt (of 524508 attempts)
    631 retransmit timeouts
        2 connections dropped by rexmit timeout
    4 persist timeouts
    641 keepalive timeouts
        340 keepalive probes sent
        68 connections dropped by keepalive
udp:
    0 incomplete headers
    0 bad data length fields
    0 bad checksums
    0 socket buffer overflows
```

```
$ netstat -s -p udp

udp:
      0 incomplete headers
      0 bad data length fields
      0 bad checksums
      0 socket buffer overflows
```

Figure 7. Network statistics for the udp **protocol**

A large number of redirect messages sent indicates that the remote hosts in the network are not using optimal routes to reach the destination host. Possibly, the remote host(s) is using static routing where the local host is using dynamic routing.

ICMP: Internet Control Message Protocol

Bad checksums and lengths are an indication of hardware failure or software failure. The software failure can be in the application layer for the ICMP protocol because applications can create ICMP datagrams directly.

TCP: Transmission Control Protocol

The first part of the TCP data shows the number of packets sent. The two values that are most useful, from a debugging standpoint, are the number of data packets retransmitted and the number of window update packets. If these values are increasing rapidly, TCP is timing out packets sent and adjusting its send window size, indicating either network traffic is too high for acknowledgements (ACKs) to return before timeout, or the receive window is too large for the network bandwidth. A high number of window probe packets may indicate that a remote peer is not reading data fast enough or at all.

The second part of the TCP data relates to TCP packets the host receives. A high number of duplicate ACKs with a high number of duplicate packets has the same indications as in the first part. A large number of out-of-order packets indicates that packets are taking different routes in the network to get from source host to destination host. Either multiple routes exist for packets to take or the routes available for packets are changing rapidly.

A large number of window updates means either the remote receiver's buffers are filling up, indicating that the remote side cannot keep up with the incoming data, or the remote side has detected congestion in the network.

```
Example output of ping (i.e. "pg /tmp/iptrace.out"):
=====( packet transmitted on interface tr0 )=====Tue Jul 4 08:23:35 1995
802.5 packet

802.5 MAC header:
access control field = 0, frame control field = 40
[src = 90:00:5a:a8:39:34, dst = 10:00:5a:4f:55:b2]
routing control field = 0840, 3 routing segments
routing segments [2291 c211 2300]
802.2 LLC header:
dsap aa, ssap aa, ctrl 3, proto 0:0:0, type 800 (IP)
IP header breakdown:
    < SRC =  129.35.31.108 > (majestic.austin.ibm.com)
    < DST =  129.35.16.87 > (smoke.austin.ibm.com)
    ip_v=4, ip_hl=20, ip_tos=0, ip_len=556, ip_id=50559, ip_off=184
    ip_ttl=255, ip_sum=c18f, ip_p = 1 (ICMP)


Example output of telnet ACK (i.e. "pg /tmp/iptrace.out"):

=====( packet received on interface tr0 )=====Tue Jul 4 08:28:34 1995
802.5 packet

802.5 MAC header:
access control field = 18, frame control field = 40
[src = 90:00:5a:4f:55:b2, dst = 10:00:5a:a8:39:34]
routing control field = 08c0, 3 routing segments
routing segments [2291 c211 2300]
802.2 LLC header:
dsap aa, ssap aa, ctrl 3, proto 0:0:0, type 800 (IP)
IP header breakdown:
    < SRC =  129.35.16.87 > (smoke.austin.ibm.com)
    < DST =  129.35.31.108 > (majestic.austin.ibm.com)
    ip_v=4, ip_hl=20, ip_tos=0, ip_len=58, ip_id=37052, ip_off=0
    ip_ttl=60, ip_sum=bbf8, ip_p = 6 (TCP)
TCP header breakdown:
    <source port=23(telnet), destination port=1246 >
    th_seq=7c9d405, th_ack=c3d81c11
    th_off=5, flags<PUSH |ACK |>
    th_win=15972, th_sum=a396, th_urp=0
00000000   fffb01ff fb03fffc c8fffd1f fffa1801   |.¹..¹..³?.².....|
00000010   fff0
```

Figure 8. Example iptrace **output of** ping **and telnet ACK**

Discarded packets are an indication of either failing hardware in the network or failing kernel, TCP, or lower-layer protocol software in the network.

The final part of the TCP data relates to connections. A high number of persistant timeouts indicates that remote machines could have their receive window set to zero. The local host is probably sending data too fast to the remote host. A high number of keep-alive timeouts is an indication that a remote host(s) is not maintaining connections properly or an intermediate router has failed (or other network equipment problems).

UDP: User Data Protocol

Look in the UDP statistics for "socket buffer overflows." If it is anything other than zero, packets are probably overrunning the UDP buffer.

On machines using AIX versions prior to 3.2.5, some versions of `netstat` do not report the socket buffer overflows statistic. But `crash` can provide the same information. As the root, invoke `crash`. At the > prompt, issue the crash sub-command: `knlist udpstat`. This command will return information in the form:

```
udpstat: 0xXXXXXXXX
```

where XXXXXXXX is a hex address. Then issue the command `od 0xXXXXXXXX 7`.

`iptrace` (or `tcpdump` in V4)

The `iptrace` command starts a daemon that records every frame a network adapter sends and receives on a specific machine. Compare this information with a network analyzer, which records every frame transmitted on a network, regardless of which machine sent/received it. In other words, if machine A runs the `iptrace` daemon, it will record all the frames it sends and receives; it will not record any of the frames machines B and C exchange. The following steps describe how to run `iptrace`, using `srcmaster`.

ETHERNET STATISTICS (en0) :
Hardware Address: 02:60:8c:2f:83:dc
Transmit Byte Count: 553000.0
Transmit Frame Count: 5945.0
Transmit Error Count: 0
Max Netid's In Use: 7
Max Receives Queued: 0
Interrupts Lost: 0
Timeout Ints Lost: 0
Receive Packets Lost: 0
No Mbuf Extension Errors: 0
Transmit Int Count: 5947
Align Error Count: 0
Packets Too Short: 0
No Resources Count: 0
Xmit Max Collisions: 0
Xmit Underrun Count: 0
Xmit Timeouts: 0
Diag Overflow Count: 0
Execute Cmd Errors: 0
Adpt Side End Of List Bit: 0
Adapter Pkts Uploaded: 8620
Receive DMA Timeouts(lock up): 0

Receive Byte Count: 439944.0
Receive Frame Count: 4310.0
Receive Error Count: 0
Max Transmits Queued: 1
Max Stat Blks Queued: 0
WDT Interrupts Lost: 0
Status Lost: 0
No Mbuf Errors: 0
Receive Int Count: 4310
CRC Error Count: 0
Recv Overrun Count: 0
Packets Too Long: 0
Recv Pkts Discarded: 0
Xmit Carrier Lost: 0
Xmit CTS Lost Count: 0
Parity Errors: 0
Execute Q Overflows: 0
Host Side End Of List Bit: 0
Adapter Pkts To Be Uploaded: 4310
Start Receptions To Adpt: 0

TOKEN STATISTICS (tr0):
Hardware Address: 10:00:5a:a8:84:ae
Transmit Byte Count: 608449186.0
Transmit Frame Count: 1157759.0 ·
Transmit Error Count: 0
Max Netid's In Use: 1
Max Receives Queued: 0
Interrupts Lost: 0
Timeout Ints Lost: 0
Receive Packets Lost: 0
No Mbuf Extension Errors: 0
Transmit Int Count: 1157741
Packets Accepted Valid NetID: 1751345
Packets Transmitted and Adapter Errors Detected: 0

Receive Byte Count: 274878085.0
Receive Frame Count: 1751345.0
Receive Error Count: 0
Max Transmits Queued: 0
Max Stat Blks Queued: 0
WDT Interrupts Lost: 0
Status Lost: 0
No Mbuf Errors: 0
Receive Int Count: 2408906
Packets Rejected No NetID: 657567
Overflow Packets Received: 0

Figure 9. Statistics for the IBM token-ring adapter device driver

1. Issue the command `chssys -s iptrace -a "-a -i tr0 -b -d <hostname>/tmp/iptrace.log`

   `-a` means "suppress arp packets"
   `-i tr0` means "trace the `tr0` token-ring interface"
   `-d <hostname>` means "trace packets to <hostname>"
   `-b` means "trace packets from <hostname>"
   `/tmp/iptrace.log` means "store the results in `/tmp/iptrace.log`"

   Other useful options:
   `-p`   specifies a port
   `-P`   specifies a protocol

2. Issue the command `startsrc -s iptrace`.

3. Initiate client/server programs on <hostname> (*e.g.*, `ping <hostname>` or whatever command or event you want to trace/debug).

4. Issue the command `stopsrc -s iptrace`.

5. Run `ipreport /tmp/iptrace.log > /tmp/iptrace.out`.

Diagnosis — How to Interpret an `ipreport`:
Put simply, `ipreport` records the TCP/IP message formats and protocols in exhaustive detail. The key to understanding an `ipreport` is knowing the structure of the IP, TCP, and UDP headers. For a detailed explanation of all these different header fields, consult the appropriate RFC. The TCP/IP chapter in the *System Management Guide: Communications and Networks*, SC23-2526, also has a good explanation of the header fields.

`netstat -v` (or `tokstat`, `entstat`, `fddistat -d` in AIX V4)
Netstat is a program that accesses network related data structures within the kernel, then provides an ASCII format at the terminal. Netstat can provide reports on the routing table, TCP connections, TCP and UDP "listens," and protocol memory management. The `-v` option retrieves device driver statistics.

```
$ ping -c1 -R smoke
PING smoke.austin.ibm.com: (129.35.16.87): 56 data bytes
64 bytes from 129.35.16.87: icmp_seq=0 ttl=255 time=12 ms
RR:    smoke.austin.ibm.com (129.35.16.87)
       hyper.austin.ibm.com (129.35.25.152)

----smoke.austin.ibm.com PING Statistics----
1 packets transmitted, 1 packets received, 0% packet loss
round-trip min/avg/max = 12/12/12 ms
```

Figure 10. An example of a ping -R **request**

Diagnosis: In the `netstat` reports, look particularly for "No Resources Counts" or "No Mbuf Errors" messages. Any counts that are very large — except byte count, frame count, and interrupt count — may indicate problems (deferred packets, excessive broadcast packets, *etc.*).

Calculate collisions as a percentage of output packets, using the following:

Xmit(timeouts + collisions)/Transmit Frame count

The network should be considered for reorganization if the collision value exceeds 15 percent.

netpmon

`netpmon` reports on the following system activities:

CPU Usage

`netpmon` monitors CPU usage due to all processes and interrupt handlers. It estimates how much of this usage is due to network-related activities and how much of the idle time is due to various types of network I/O.

Network Device-Driver I/O

`netpmon` monitors I/O operations through all Ethernet and token-ring network device-drivers. In the case of transmission I/O, it also monitors utilizations, queue lengths, and destination hosts.

Internet Socket Calls

`netpmon` monitors all `send`, `recv`, `sendto`, `recvfrom`, `read`, and `write` system calls on Internet sockets. It reports statistics on a per-process basis for each protocol type (TCP, UDP, ICMP, *etc.*).

NFS I/O

`netpmon` monitors read/write system calls on client Network File System (NFS) files, client NFS remote procedure call (RPC) requests, and NFS server read/write requests. It reports system call statistics on a per-process basis and on a per-file basis for each server. `netpmon` reports client RPC statistics for each server and server read/write statistics for each client.

```
$ ping -s 2000 smoke
PING smoke.austin.ibm.com: (129.35.16.87): 2000 data bytes
2008 bytes from 129.35.16.87: icmp_seq=0 ttl=255 time=14 ms
2008 bytes from 129.35.16.87: icmp_seq=1 ttl=255 time=14 ms
2008 bytes from 129.35.16.87: icmp_seq=2 ttl=255 time=15 ms
2008 bytes from 129.35.16.87: icmp_seq=3 ttl=255 time=15 ms
¬C
----smoke.austin.ibm.com PING Statistics----
7 packets transmitted, 7 packets received, 0% packet loss
round-trip min/avg/max = 14/14/16 ms
```

Figure 11. An example of a `ping -s` **report**

You can specify any combination of the above system activity reports by using the command line flags. If no combination is specified, all the reports are produced.

Diagnosis: The `netpmon` report is very lengthy. Its two most important functions are to identify MTU fragmentation and show host traffic.

`netpmon` can help identify MTU fragmentation since the average, maximum, minimum, and standard deviation of packet sizes are shown in the detailed section.

`netpmon` also shows host traffic at the device, TCP, and UDP layers. It can detect traffic to other networks and display network traffic statistics sorted by host. If hosts appearing in the device section of the `netpmon` report do not appear in the TCP section, the host is an intermediary.

`ping -R` (or `traceroute`)

The `ping` command sends an echo request to a network host. The `-R` flag specifies the record route option. Returned packets display the route buffer. It is important to note that the IP header is only large enough for nine such routes. Also, many hosts and gateways ignore this option.

Figure 10 shows an example of a `ping -R` request. The `-c 1` flag specifies that ping should send only one request.

Diagnosis: Document the intermediate hosts to record the route packets are taking through the network. Also record/compare round-trip times and packet loss statistics through various routes. If the ping line displays immediately but the ping command does not return, the problem is a network problem, not a name resolution problem.

`ping -s`: Average Round-Trip Time

To obtain information about a host and specify the number of data bytes to be sent, add the `-s` flag to the ping command (`ping -s 2000 <hostname>`), or simply follow the command with the packet size (`ping <hostname> 2000`). Figure 11 provides an example of a `ping -s` report.

$ netstat -I tr0 5									
input (tr0) output					input (total) output				
packets	errs	packets	errs	colls	packets	errs	packets	errs	colls
1820357	0	1171111	0	0	1825849	0	1178326	0	0
59	0	6	0	0	59	0	6	0	0
157	0	9	0	0	157	0	9	0	0
64	0	8	0	0	64	0	8	0	0
54	0	6	0	0	54	0	6	0	0
52	0	6	0	0	52	0	6	0	0
84	0	14	0	0	84	0	14	0	0

Figure 12. An example of the network load in packets per second

Diagnosis: Note the difference in round-trip times between a `ping` issue with the correct packet size and one that is larger.

Run an `iptrace` to verify packets are fragmented. Search the output of `ipreport` to see if the "more fragments" bit is set in the IP header flags field.

`netstat -I tr0 5`: Network Load In Packets/Second

The `netstat -I` command can provide a rough idea of the network load in packets per second as Figure 12 shows.

Diagnosis: Analyze the network load during both peak and idle times. Use this data to balance the mbuf pool sizes in AIX V3. Otherwise, this data provides a good estimation of bandwidth usage by node and IP protocol.

Conclusion

Steps 5 and 6 illustrate the fact that it is important to adopt a methodical, structured approach to problem solving. The essence of structured troubleshooting is to move from the general to the particular, so that as details become finer, more possibilities are eliminated. As Sherlock Holmes said, "When you have eliminated the impossible whatever remains, however improbable, must be the truth." Of course, for this to be valid, you must have considered all of the possibilities. Holmes also said, "It is a capital mistake to theorize before one has data." This chapter has enabled you to capture the data. Part 3 will provide suggestions for analyzing it.

References

[1] Hunt, Craig. *TCP/IP Network Administration*, ISBN 0-937175-82-X, O'Reilly and Associates, Inc., September 1993.

[2] IBM Corp. *Introduction to Performance in Router Networks*, 1st Edition, IBM Publication GG24-4223-00, International Technical Support Organization, 1993.

[3] IBM Corp. *AIX Performance Tuning Guide*, 4th Edition, IBM Publication SC23-2365-03, 1994.

Sam Nokes
IBM Corporation
11400 Burnet Road
Austin, TX 78758
snokes@vnet.ibm.com

As a member of IBM's National
Technical Support Organization,
the AIX Systems Center, Mr. Nokes
provides AIX Communication and
Network Performance support. He
has more than six years of UNIX
communications programming and
support experience.

10 Steps to Improve AIX TCP/IP Network Performance – Part 3

By Sam Nokes

This chapter is the last of a three-part series providing detailed steps on improving your AIX TCP/UDP/IP network performance on RISC System/6000s. This chapter discusses global principles of communication tuning with a focus on TCP, UDP, and IP protocols.

The first two parts of this series discussed how to determine if there is a problem with your TCP/IP/UDP network, how to determine what tools to use, and how to collect the data. The last part of this series will explain how to analyze the data and tune your network for better performance.

Step 7: Turn Performance Data Into Information — Analyze It

Most IT professionals are familiar with the situation of having lots of data, but no real information. Information comes from the analysis of the data. This chapter will give you some helpful hints to turn the data from your AIX performance tools into valuable information.

AIX Communication Subsystem Memory (mbuf) Management

`netstat -m`

At times, you may see the network use 90 percent or more of the available resources. This number is a percentage of what is allocated, not a percentage of the system maximum (`thewall`). Therefore, 90 percent usage does not necessarily mean congestion. It means that either the user or the system should allocate more mbufs upon demand.

Root may use the network options `no` command to modify the mbuf pool parameters, which affect the size of the mbuf pools and how they are managed. With AIX 3.2, the user can increase allocation by setting `lowclust` higher.

The `netstat -m` report can be compared to the existing system parameters by issuing the command `no -a`, which reports all of the current settings.

The following are some guidelines for managing mbuf pools on AIX 3.2: One-fourth of the physical memory should be available for communication buffers (mbufs). Setting the upper limit (`thewall`) at that point does not eat up memory as it is not consumed unless it is required. If the memory size is X (in KB), set the following values to the mbuf pool parameters:

```
no -o thewall=X/4
no -o mb_cl_hiwat=X/32
no -o lowclust=X/64
no -o lowmbuf=X/64
```

Note that X is expressed in KB. So, for 16 MB of memory, X=16,384 KB.

1. After expanding the pools, use the vmstat command to ensure paging rates have not increased. If it is not possible to expand the pools to the necessary levels without adversely affecting the paging rates, additional memory may be required.

2. When adjusting lowclust, adjust lowmbuf by at least the same amount. For every large mbuf there will exist a small mbuf that points to it.

3. mb_cl_hiwat should remain at least two times greater than lowclust at all times. This level will prevent netm thrashing.

4. When adjusting lowclust and lowmbuf, thewall may need to be increased to prevent pool expansions from exceeding the limit.

NOTE: AIX Version 4 has done away with most of the mbuf tuning options with a goal of making the communication memory management system "self-tuning." The two items that remain are thewall and sb_max, and they have the same purposes as in AIX Version 3.2.

Basically, AIX 4.1.0 and later starts with a fixed size and adds more mbufs as needed and then slowly frees them back to the system if the count is above the high water mark. The fact that netm frees the mbufs slowly will handle any peak needs and not return them until the demand for that size mbuf goes down. AIX 4.1 also uses variable clusters, so clusters can now be 1, 2, 4, 8, or 16 KB (not just 4 KB).

Application Layer

At the application layer, the size of the buffer written to the socket is very important in achieving the highest throughput for a particular interface. On AIX 3.2, try to use a size that is a multiple of 4 KB, since that value is the size of a page and of a cluster. Small packets (less than 4 KB) will degrade TCP throughput of the LAN adapter.

Writing 936 bytes on AIX 3.2 would result in 3,160 bytes of wasted space per write. The application could hit the udp_recvspace (explained later) default value of 65,536 bytes with just 16 writes totaling 14,976 bytes of data. If the application were using TCP, this would waste time as well as memory. For AIX 4.1, the crossover point is 228 bytes.

Recall that TCP tries to form outbound data into Maximum Transmission Unit (MTU)-sized packets. If the MTU of the LAN were larger than 14,976 bytes, TCP would put the sending thread to sleep when the tcp_sendspace limit was reached. The receiver would have to get a timeout ACK to force the data to be written.

Users should note that with AIX Version 3 the performance of odd-sized writes is lower, and they use more CPU. This result is due to the TCP/IP Internet checksum routine not being optimized for odd byte sizes. This problem is fixed in AIX 4.1. So, where possible, don't send odd byte size messages on 3.2.x systems.

Socket Layer

Socket send or receive buffer sizes are limited to no more than sb_max bytes, because sb_max is a ceiling on buffer space consumption.

The two quantities are not measured in the same way, however. The socket buffer size limits the amount of data that the socket buffers can hold. sb_max limits the number of bytes of mbufs that the socket buffer can hold at any given time.

In an AIX 3.2 Ethernet environment, for example, each 4,096-byte mbuf cluster might hold just 1,500 bytes of data. The main problem is that this mbuf cluster size counts as 4 KB against the sb_max limit. So, if you receive an 8 KB datagram on Ethernet, it is really 8,192 bytes divided by 1,500 bytes, which is six packets. These six packets will consume six clusters, which is 6 X 4 KB or 24 KB of socket buffer. (These six packets need six small mbufs as well.) Thus, sb_max would have to be 2.73 times larger than the specified socket buffer size to allow the buffer to reach its specified capacity.

The value of sb_max can be displayed with the command no -a and set (by root) with the command no -o sb_max=NewLimit. The change will take effect immediately for new connections but is effective only until the next system boot. To carry the change across system boot, place the command in the file /etc/rc.net.

TCP/UDP Layer

Network options (viewed with the no command) tcp_sendspace and tcp_recvspace define the buffer sizes for stream sockets and thus the TCP window size, *e.g.*, how much data TCP can send before it needs an acknowledgement. The total can be spread over several packets (*i.e.*, TCP segments), where the MTU bounds the packet/segment size.

UDP send and receive spaces serve the same purpose as their TCP counterparts. Since UDP has no sliding window feature, shortage of buffer space will have a detrimental effect: loss of data. If an application retransmits these data, the result is a decrease in effective throughput. TCP and UDP send and receive space values can be displayed with the no -a command and set (by root) with the command no -o tcp_recvspace=NewValue. The NewValue parameter must be less than or equal to the sb_max parameter, which controls the maximum amount of space that a

socket's send or receive buffer can use. The optimal value for
`tcp_sendspace` and `tcp_recvspace` is computed as follows:

```
optimal value = media bandwidth *
  average round trip time
```

For media bandwidth, use the values:

```
Token-Ring (4 Mbps)
  4,194,304 (1,024 * 1,024 * 4)
Ethernet (10 Mbps)
  10,485,760 (1,024 * 1,024 * 10)
Token-Ring (16 Mbps)
  16,777,216 (1,024 * 1,024 * 16)
```

Average round trip time is extracted from `ping -s size -c count
hostname`. (See chapter x for sample output.)

For example, on a 10 Mbit per second Ethernet with a maximum
round trip of 14 ms, the calculation would be:

```
maximum window = 14ms * 1.25
  MB/second = 17,500 bytes
```

The window cannot become larger than this value, so the TCP receive
space is set to 17,500 bytes.

The `no` parameter named `RFC1323` enables the use of the high-
performance TCP feature. Essentially, this stipulation allows the send
and receive socket buffer sizes, which translate into the TCP send and
receive window sizes, to be set to values exceeding the previous
maximum of 64 KB. The usefulness of this feature is evident in
benchmark testing on the RISC System/6000 Model 590 where the
maximum FDDI throughput was obtained at a TCP window size of
128 KB, which would not have been possible without this feature.

IP Layer

At the IP layer, the only tunable parameter is `ipqmaxlen`, which controls the length of the IP input queue and exists only in AIX Version 3. (For a discussion of `ipqmaxlen`, see part two of this series.) The maximum length of this queue is set using the `no` command. For example, `no -o ipqmaxlen=100` allows 100 packets to be queued up. The maximum burst rate received determines the exact value to use. However, if the maximum burst rate cannot be determined, using the number of overflows can help determine what the increase should be. Increasing the queue length does not use additional memory, but it could mean that more time will be spent in the off-level interrupt handler as IP will have more packets to process on its input queue. This situation could adversely affect processes needing CPU time. The trade-off is reduced packet dropping versus CPU availability for other processing. It is best to increase `ipqmaxlen` by moderate increments if the above trade-off is a concern.

One other consideration with IP is dropped fragments. If the `netstat -s -p ip` field, "fragment dropped after timeout," is non-zero, fragments of an incomplete datagram were discarded after the `ipfragttl` time (specified by `no`). The fragments may not have been received for a number of reasons: network errors, lack of mbufs, or transmit overruns. The default `ipfragttl` is 60 seconds. Increasing this value may be of benefit on a congested network.

Interface Layer

At the interface (IF) layer, the MTU is the important parameter. For the best throughput for systems on the same type of network, it is advisable to use the defaults, with the exception being the token-ring (TR) interfaces. Increase the MTU on 4 Mb TR interfaces to 4,056 bytes and increase 16 Mb interfaces to 8,500 bytes in place of the default values. Because all systems on a LAN must have the same

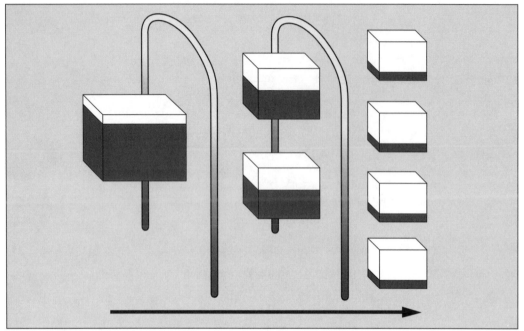

Figure 1. MTU Packet Fragmentation

MTU, they must all change simultaneously. The change will be effective across boots. For the loopback interface `lo0` in AIX Version 3.2.5, increase the value to 16,896 bytes.

The demands of an application will usually be the basis for defining the optimum packet size. For example, an application may ask for data in large segments, probably spanning several network packets. In this instance, it would be best to set the maximum frame size to what the network protocol allows (1,518 bytes in the case of Ethernet). This size would reduce the number of packets required for the data transfer and minimize the effect of the protocol overheads.

In multi-network environments, where data may travel from a network with a large MTU to a network with a smaller MTU, fragmentation can occur. The large IP packets must be broken into smaller packets by the router, so the small-MTU network can transmit them, which will cause the receiving system CPU time to reassemble the fragmented packets, thus reducing throughput, as Figure 1 illustrates.

The solution is to reduce the larger MTU to the same size as the smaller using the command `chdev -l interface -a mtu=NewValue`. This command will stop the fragmentation but will also reduce the point-to-point throughput between systems on the large MTU network.

TCP in AIX sets a conservative value of 512 bytes for the maximum segment size (MSS) when the destination host is on a different, remote network. The MSS is related to the MTU. The default TCP segment size can be found in `/usr/include/netinet/tcp.h` near the end of the file. The message reads: "With an IP MSS of 576, this is 536 (576 - 40 byte TCP/IP headers), but 512 is probably more convenient." While this default is appropriate for the general Internet, it can be

TCP/IP and LAN Performance with Respect to AIX 4.1.0 and 4.1.1

AIX 4.1.0 performance exceeds 3.2.5 performance as noted in the following table. **NOTE:** 4.1.0 code is SMP enabled (more locks).

This table reflects the Geometric Mean of all tests run on all media (Ethernet, token-ring, FDDI, loopback, and AF_UNIX loopback) and the results are scaled for CPU utilization.

Geometric Mean Comparison of AIX 4.1.0 to AIX 3.2.5

TEST	MACHINE MODEL		
	580 (RS1)	59H (RS2)	C10 (601)
Netperf	109%	116%	117%
FTP file xfer	159%	162%	136%

Specific 4.1.0 TCP/IP performance improvements included:

1. Improved internet checksum routine (`in_cksum`) that improved even byte checksum time by 30 percent and improved odd byte length packets by 1,230 percent.

2. FTP file transfer in ASCII mode was improved by using assembly routines to handle the scanning of the data. ASCII mode file transfers on FDDI are twice as fast now on AIX 4.1.0.

3. The LAN drivers have removed one layer of "off-level" processing, so they are more streamlined.

4. Lots of work to recover performance lost in moving to the OSF TCP/IP source code (which was SMP enabled). This move required lots of changes to locking routines and a list of changes too numerous to list here.

5. A number of changes in the AIX kernel also helped. For example, the GLINK overhead is now removed on the most commonly used primitives called by kernel extensions. Improvements to the SMP locking routines were made.

6. IBM also has improved network and adapter statistics. These can also all be cleared (zeroed), which is helpful in troubleshooting and testing.

There was just a short time period between the 4.1.0 release and the 4.1.1 release, so only minor changes were made for 4.1.1. These changes were mainly to the sockets layer and TCP/IP.

1. Hashing of Protocol Control Blocks (PCBs) to reduce search time when large numbers of sockets/session are open (like TCP-A or C).

2. Variable size clusters. Mbuf clusters are no longer confined to 4 KB — As part of the sockets memory allocator, clusters can be any size that is a power of two up to 16 KB. Performance improves because one 8 KB cluster instead of two 4 KB clusters can be used, for example, or one 512 byte cluster instead of three smaller mbufs. In addition, less memory is used for buffers. This change resulted in a 6 percent improvement of the geometric mean of all tests.

3. Internet checksum computation "on the fly" during the copy of the data into the kernel. For 4.1.1, this option is being done for UDP datagrams. This code has been measured and given a 9 percent improvement.

unnecessarily restrictive for private internets within an administrative domain. In such an environment, MTU sizes of the component physical networks are known, and the administrator can determine minimum MTU and optimal MSS. AIX provides several ways in which TCP can use this optimal MSS. Both source and destination hosts must support these features. In a heterogeneous, multi-vendor environment, the availability of the feature on both systems may determine the choice of the solution. See "Tuning TCP Maximum Segment Size (MSS)" in the *AIX Performance Guide* for a more comprehensive discussion of the MSS options that follow [1]:

1. Specify a static route to a specific remote network using the
   -mtu option of the route command to specify the MTU to that network.

2. Use the tcp_mssdflt option of the no command.

3. Use subnetting and the subnetsarelocal option of the no command.

Device Driver Layer
At the device driver layer, you can configure both the transmit and receive queues. It is possible to overrun these queues. The command netstat -v will show Max Transmits queued and Max Receives queued. If these values are close to the value of their respective lengths (use lsattr -E -l device to see the queue lengths), then you should increase the queues. Another indication that the transmit queue is being overrun is if the netstat -i command reports values greater than 0 in the Oerr column, as mentioned in Part 2. (Oerr stands for Outgoing error and is an indication that the IF layer received an error when it called the device driver.)

Regardless of your tuning priorities, you should always set
xmt_que_size to the maximum — 150. This setting does not
consume any additional space unless the memory is really needed
for data. The appropriate command is # chdev -l ifname -a
xmt_que_size=150, where ifname is the name of the interface
(*i.e.*, tok0, en0, etc.). If the LAN adapter is already in use, you must
take it offline temporarily to change this parameter.

For a token-ring adapter, for example, the appropriate sequence
of commands would be:

```
# ifconfig tr0 detach
# chdev -l tok0 -a xmt_que_size=150
# ifconfig tr0 hostname up
```
(hostname is the TCP/IP hostname for your system)

SMIT can do the same thing, entering through the devices menus to do
Change/Show on the appropriate network adapter. The rec_que_size
is tuneable only in AIX Version 3 and should be set to 150 as a matter
of course on network-oriented systems, especially servers.

Another parameter to check at the device driver level is the Receive
Data Transfer Offset (RDTO) field that indicates where in the receive
buffer the packet data actually begins (smit chgtok). RDTO is
primarily an AIX internal performance enhancement method. The
basic idea is to leave enough room in front of the data to allow the
maximum possible header, which may need to be prepended. This
action prevents copying data from buffer to buffer as headers are
added. It does not affect the receive buffers on the adapter but is
used only in system memory.

Primarily, RDTO was used, so SNA could easily prepend an
Inter-Process Communication (IPC) header. But, it also has
implications for IP routing. Consider a packet arriving on the

Ethernet. The 14-byte header is removed and the packet is passed to IP. IP decides to forward it out to token-ring. The token-ring header size can be only up to 40 bytes. There is no room to prepend the token header (only 14 free bytes), so a new mbuf must be chained to the front. If the Ethernet RDTO was 26 bytes, then the entire TR header could have been prepended:

```
Ethernet        26
   Ethernet_rdto 26 + Ethernet_header 14 = 40
Token-ring       0
   Token_Ring_rdto 0 + Token_Ring_header 40 = 40
802.3           18
   8023_rdto 18 + 8023_header 22 = 40
X.25            12
   x25_rdto 12 + x25_pseudo_header 28 = 40
```

So, the values recommended are for forwarding packets. If the RS/6000 is not a gateway and is not using SNA, RDTOs of zero probably make sense. Actually, an RDTO of 2 would be best for Ethernet since that value would word align everything after the Ethernet header.

Step 8: Handle Performance Problems

An easy way to tell if the network is affecting overall performance is to compare those operations that involve the network with those that do not. If you are running a program that does a considerable amount of remote reads and writes and it is running slowly, but everything else seems to be running normally, then it is probably a network problem. For example, with Network File System (NFS), try logging onto the remote system directly and use its files, or localize the files to eliminate the NFS configuration and code issues. Logging onto the system directly avoids the NFS configuration, thus isolating the problem. For example, a user experiences slow response time when reading a file that is part of an NFS mounted filesystem. By logging onto the NFS server directly, she issues the same command and gets better performance. The problem is now isolated to the network of the NFS configuration.

Once you've uncovered a network performance problem, what are your options?

1. Program Temporary Fixes (PTFs) — Get the Latest

Your first course of action should be to call 1-800-237-5511 and request the latest cumulative PTF for the communication subsystems device drivers, etc. There's nothing more frustrating than to spend days in analysis only to find a PTF is the resolution. Best to head this situation off at the pass and update to the latest PTF (if possible) before beginning analysis.

To give you a taste of the potential for PTF resolution, consider the following:

◆ There were some massive retransmit/hang/crash system problems with the Ethernet card/driver combinations in the early part of 1992. You should consider this circumstance when using any old adapters.

◆ If you have a machine running with the integrated Ethernet adapter (220, 340, 350), make sure you have PTF U418311 (IX33836) installed.

And while on the subject of upgrading, you might want to consider an upgrade to AIX Version 4. AIX 4.1 TCP performance exceeds 3.2.5 performance as noted in the related sidebar (see page 78).

DEVICE	ISO LAYER	PERFORMANCE FACTOR
Repeaters	Physical Layer	No help with performance
Bridges	Data Link Layer	Must limit some traffic to help
Routers	Network Layer	Divides networks logically by IP address Can isolate traffic to improve performance
Gateways	Application Layer	Same as router to aid in performance Slower handling multi-network traffic

Figure 2. Effect of Connection Devices on Network Performance

2. Upgrade Resources

Upgrading the links between end-hosts (higher bandwidth)
or upgrading the end-hosts/internetwork hosts (faster CPU,
memory, and disk) is an obvious way to handle performance
problems. In fact, this approach is used quite often in today's
networks running devices and lines on a low utilization.
Nevertheless, this approach is costly, and it might be
worthwhile to investigate other solutions first.

3. Tuning

Tuning issues should be considered both initially, when a network
is designed, and regularly while the network is running. The
necessity to review tuning parameters could be triggered by the
problem management discipline (users are unsatisfied with the
performance of the network). It could also be triggered by
information obtained through the monitoring process (for
example, recognizing a high fragmentation/reassembling rate).

4. Load Balancing

Depending on the product and the implementation, internetworking
devices such as routers might have features that could be used to
address performance issues. Load balancing is one such feature.

Some routers do support transmission groups, that is, multiple
communication lines are grouped together and appear as one.
The router will use all individual lines and provide the aggregated
bandwidth to the higher layers.

Another way of load balancing is implemented in the Open
Shortest Path First (OSPF), a standard routing protocol for IP traffic
(though not necessarily implemented by all routers). If configured
appropriately, it will distribute the traffic onto different communication
lines. If, for example, two routers are connected by two leased lines,
the individual packets would be sent in an alternating fashion:

one packet over the first line, the next packet over the second line, and so on.

5. Prioritization

Some routers can give one protocol stack higher priority than the rest, which may avoid situations where an interactive user is being affected by a concurrent file transfer. Unfortunately, prioritization is not a standard feature. Implementations of different vendors are usually incompatible and vary in functionality.

Applying a mechanism such as prioritization does not always solve a performance problem. Often these mechanisms work on a packet level rather than on a bit or byte level (one packet A and then three packets B). If you want to prioritize one protocol stack over another and the protocols have very different packet sizes, then on a byte level you may not achieve the desired result.

6. Redesigning the Network

Sometimes the best way to address a performance problem is to redesign the network or parts of the network. It makes sense sometimes to rearrange routers and bridges or the way they are interconnected, in order to adapt the network structure to the traffic flow. Enter the principle of segmentation/partitioning. The most effective way of getting the best out of the available bandwidth of the network is by partitioning the network so that traffic is confined to the areas where it is needed and excluded from the areas where it is not relevant. The way to do this is to implement bridges and routers.

Superficially, bridges and routers do similar tasks — they analyze network data and decide where to send the traffic. The difference is the way they do this. A bridge is a device that operates at the datalink layer (Layer 2 of the seven-layer OSI model), while a router works at the network layer (Layer 3). An easy way to distinguish the two: bridges to filter, routers to isolate.

Each approach has its advantages and disadvantages. For instance, since a router works at the network level, it can route traffic according to protocol type and protocol contents (such as an IP address); however, it must read and decode the frame to the network layer, which necessarily will affect the throughput of the device.

By contrast, a bridge does not need to decode the frame, but only to read the Ethernet header and Layer 2 information. While this leads to a higher throughput, it also means that it can only route traffic by physical addresses (which are contained in the header information). The design requirements of the two device types are therefore different.

The bridge will be attached to a number of networks and must examine every packet on each of the attached networks. A router need only examine packets that have been sent there. Thus, a bridge will need high performance hardware (such as content addressable memory), and a router will require powerful processors (such as RISC).

Until quite recently, throughput requirements often dictated the choice between bridge or router; however, recent developments in microprocessor technology have meant that router throughput has increased considerably.

Hybrid products — called brouters — have emerged that offer the facilities of both devices. A brouter will route traffic according to network information where it can and will bridge other traffic. For example, a brouter may route all TCP/IP traffic according to IP address but route all other traffic according to the physical node address of the destination [2]. Figure 2 compares the performance of repeaters, bridges, routers, and gateways.

A good rule of thumb is that networks that show a steady load above 15 percent will benefit from some form of filtering or restructuring with bridges or routers or by relocating some workstations. If the load is 25 percent or higher for more than just transient peaks, then the network will not be functioning well. If the traffic is running at this 25 percent level, you should reduce the traffic and see if the reported problems are resolved. The command `netstat -v` will provide the following information on the transmit error percentage: `Xmit(timeouts +collisions) /Transmit Frame count > 15%`. In other words, collisions as a percentage of output packets `> 15%` indicate that the network should be considered for reorganization to balance the load.

Seriously consider reorganizing your network when:

♦ Average network utilization > 35 percent

♦ Peak network utilization   > 55 percent

♦ Average collision rate   > 10 percent

As previously mentioned, segmenting is the easiest and most common way of providing a network with more bandwidth. For example, divide a 100-user Ethernet network into two 50-user networks, thus doubling the bandwidth available to users.

Ethernet switching has emerged as a variation on segmenting. Switching relies on a different network design than traditional Ethernet networks. Ethernet LANs supply one 10-Mb/s LAN that all users share. Switching provides users with access to a central wiring hub that can operate at multiple gigabits per second so more bandwidth is available to users. A network technician then divides this bandwidth among users and can even configure switched Ethernet networks so each user receives his or her own 10-Mb/s LAN. [3]

In other words, these two communicating nodes have been removed from the shared media network where other nodes are competing for bandwidth and placed on their own private LAN for a temporary period (as long as necessary to deliver a frame). This "dedicated" LAN is virtual in that it exists only as long as necessary to deliver the frame. The switch improves performance by increasing aggregate throughput and connection latency, decreasing the error or collision rate, and also typically decreasing the lost packet count.

Step 9: Reduce the Static — Tune Your Network Environment

In general, you should do performance tuning when you want to improve the price/performance ratio of your system. Possible specific goals might be:

◆ To send more files across the network in a given day without buying more hardware or using more processor time

◆ To pass data more quickly between two specific host computers

◆ To lower the TCP/IP overhead on an application

The following guidelines should help you develop your overall approach to TCP/IP performance tuning [4].

Performance Tuning is a Reallocation of Resources

Carefully choose your tuning objectives. The way you tune to improve one resource might affect the way the network uses one or more other resources. For example, when you reduce the CPU utilization, storage consumption might increase. Before you begin tuning, have a clear idea of which of your resources you are running out of and which still have room for growth.

Law of Diminishing Returns

Your greatest performance benefits usually come from your initial

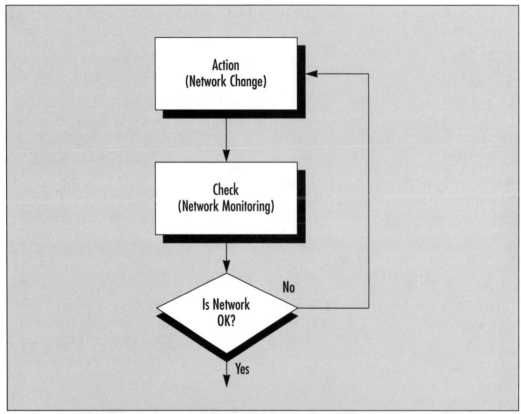

Figure 3. The Check-and-Balance Cycle. The data obtained by the monitoring process should be used to implement a "check-and-balance cycle." Every action within performance management should be followed by monitoring the network to check the results of that action.

efforts. Further changes generally produce smaller and smaller benefits and require more and more effort.

Don't Tune Just for the Sake of Tuning
Tune to relieve identified constraints. Like most anything else, you will see little benefit unless you get to the root of the problem. If what you are tuning is not the primary cause of performance problems, it will have little or no effect on response time until you have relieved the major constraints. Unnecessary tuning can actually make subsequent tuning work more difficult. If there is any significant improvement potential, it lies in improving the performance of the resources that are major factors in the response time.

Look at the Big Picture
Network performance is constrained by how far and how fast information can travel and by how many times you have to move the data. Consider the network performance as a whole, not just TCP/IP.

Change One Parameter at a Time
Do not change more than one performance tuning parameter at a time. Even if you are sure that all the changes will be beneficial, you will have no way of evaluating how much each change contributed. You also cannot effectively judge the tradeoffs resulting from each parameter change. Every time you adjust a parameter to improve one area, you almost always affect at least one other area.

Understand the Problem Before Upgrading Your Hardware
Even if it seems that more storage, processor power, or a new router could immediately improve performance, take time to understand where your bottlenecks are. You might spend the money on more storage only to find that you do not have the processing power to exploit it or the limits of the network you are crossing cannot move data any faster anyway.

Fallback Procedures

Sometimes, tuning can cause unexpected performance results. If what you have changed leads to poorer performance, you should reverse the change and try something else. If you save the former setup, then backing out the incorrect change will be much simpler.

Step 10: Review Your Changes

If there are constant changes in the network (such as adding a new host or a new application, which will change the traffic pattern in the network), you should in fact monitor the network all the time. Otherwise, your policy can spread over a longer period of time. The data obtained by the monitoring process in Step 6 should be used to implement a "check-and-balance cycle," as Figure 3 illustrates.

You should make incremental tuning changes to your configuration one at a time and test the changes to see if they have had the results you anticipated, while paying attention to sensitive resources.

To improve performance, you have to understand bottlenecks. A computer system and its applications represent a complex system of events, data routing operations, and component performance capacities. Single events or single components can create a gridlock that isn't easily perceived. Furthermore, it is possible to misrepresent the application and how it works, what it does, and the options it provides.

Sometimes the bottleneck is how an application is used. The wrong modes, commands, and techniques can spawn an excessive load when other methods will yield the same results faster. And sometimes the results are not even the correct results. Make certain, first, that you understand the process and the different paths you could take to achieve the desired results. You will achieve better optimization when you understand the interactions and have more options.

When it is clear that the options are limited, the performance of applications is best enhanced by either improving the application itself or switching software. Move from resource-intensive GUI environments to text-based applications. Critical applications and ones that are not easily replaced present a more complex problem. If possible, optimize performance by throwing hardware at the bottleneck. Know the bottleneck. Understand the effects of increased RAM. Add more RAM for larger CPU caches. Increase the size of the disk caches. Defragment hard disks, and increase the amount of free storage disks. Add hard disks or long-term storage media supporting faster seek and transfer times. Replace simple disk controllers with faster interfaces, or add multiple disks. Replace a slow system with a system that has a wider or faster bus, a faster CPU, and a faster video display. When it seems that multiple components are creating overlapping bottlenecks, avoid the trap of upgrading a computer system in small pieces and small steps; the time can be better spent evaluating the bottlenecked system and entirely replacing it with a faster platform or application [6].

Conclusion
There you have it — 10 steps to better network performance. Here's a quick recap for reference:

Step **1**: Establish a Starting Point
Step **2**: Understand the Problem
Step **3**: Devise a Plan
Step **4**: Look for Signs of Trouble
Step **5**: Select the Right Tool for the Job
Step **6**: Monitor and Collect Performance Data
Step **7**: Analyze Your Performance Data
Step **8**: Handle Performance Problems
Step **9**: Tune Your Network Environment
Step 10: Review Your Changes

Remember, complete documentation is your best tool for optimizing network performance, and if you need assistance, we're here to help. Both IBM's Availability Services Centers and the AIX Systems Center offer a portfolio of services that can bring the industry's most talented resources to your business computing problems. IBM provides services in the following AIX related areas:

◆ Performance Analysis & Tuning

◆ Migration Consulting

◆ CASE

◆ Porting Services

◆ Application Code Services

◆ Capacity Planning

◆ Customized Consulting

◆ Workshops

◆ Integration Services

◆ Analysis Tools

◆ Transaction Processing

◆ Open Systems Management

◆ Network Design and Implementation

For more information about IBM's AIX Consulting and Services offerings, call (800) CALL-AIX, or E-mail us at: `CALLAIX@.vnet.ibm.com`.

References

[1] IBM Corp. *AIX Performance Tuning Guide*, 4th Edition, IBM Publication SC23-2365-03, 1994.

[2] Theakston, Ian W. *NetWare LANs Performance and Troubleshooting*, ISBN 0-201-63175-X, Addison-Wesley Publishers, 1994.

[3] Mills, Brendon W. "Where to Turn for Network Bandwidth," *UNIX Review*, July 1995: 47-51.

[4] IBM Corp. *TCP/IP Performance Tuning Guide*, 1st Edition, IBM Publication SC31-7188-00, 1994.

[5] Nemzow, Martin A. W. *Enterprise Network Performance Optimization*, ISBN 0-07-911889-5, McGraw-Hill, Inc. 1995.

[6] DDN Network Information Center. *Tools for Monitoring and Debugging TCP/IP Internets and InterConnected Devices*, RFC 1147, April 1990.

[7] IBM Corp. *Introduction to Performance in Router Networks*, 1st Edition, IBM Publication GG24-4223-00, International Technical Support Organization, 1993.

[8] IBM Corp. *Monitoring Performance in Router Networks*, 1st Edition, IBM Publication GG24-4157-00, International Technical Support Organization, 1993.

Dennis Bordelon

Dennis Bordelon has over 20 years'
experience in product marketing,
consulting, and engineering in
networking and communications
systems. He is presently marketing
manager of PLATINUM *technology
inc.*'s Los Angeles Laboratory, located
in Inglewood, CA. Dennis holds BSEE
and MSEE degrees from the University
of Notre Dame. He can be reached
at dennisb@locus.com.

PC-to-AIX Connectivity: RISCs and Rewards

By Dennis Bordelon,
PLATINUM *technology, inc.*

What are the various means of connecting
PCs to IBM RS/6000 servers running AIX
3.2.5 and 4.1? This chapter answers the
question by addressing such topics as
terminal emulation; using TCP/IP stacks;
file/print sharing; integrating AIX with
NetWare; E-mail; and the impact of
Windows 95, Windows NT, and OS/2
Warp on AIX connectivity. In addition,
the chapter takes a look at the Distributed
Computing Environment, its Distributed
File System, and Transarc's AFS.

PC-to-AIX connectivity can be a confusing issue. For instance, what does the term PC-to-AIX connectivity mean? For some, it means either running terminal sessions over RS-232 or X/Windows over transfer control protocol/internet protocol (TCP/IP). To others, it means sharing files and printers among PCs using the RISC System/6000 (RS/6000) as a server. Still others regard it as a means of integrating RS/6000 systems into existing Novell NetWare PC local area networks (LANs).

Connectivity is a multifaceted issue with varying levels of complexity. While concentrating on RS/6000 servers, this chapter looks at the various issues in PC-to-AIX connectivity, describes the methods used to provide connectivity, and analyzes the benefits and drawbacks of each method. This information also applies to other platforms running AIX, such as Motorola, PowerPC, and some Apple servers.

Reasons for PC-to-AIX Connectivity

Before you can decide which method(s) to use for PC-to-AIX connectivity, you need to ask yourself why you need connectivity. First, consider the purpose of the AIX system and the PCs in your organization. Then, consider the level of expertise of your AIX administrator and the PC users.

RS/6000 systems are typically used to run engineering, scientific, and business applications. These advanced applications are uniquely suited to the UNIX platform because of UNIX's multiuser, multiprocess architecture and fail-safe mechanisms.

AIX systems have powerful resources at their disposal, including system resources such as large disk drives, powerful RISC processors, plenty of memory, plus CD-ROM and tape drives. AIX systems also control access to and serve as print queues to powerful printers. Therefore, not only can AIX systems run applications accessible by multiple users, but they also can share resources with PC users.

PCs run thousands of DOS and Windows personal productivity ap-plications, such as word processing and spreadsheet programs. These applications, which require modest system and printer resources, can run on inexpensive Intel processors. However, newer Windows applications place ever-increasing demands on PC re-sources. This added demand is where the need for accessing AIX resources arises.

Large corporations and other organizations use AIX systems for client/server applications such as distributed database management systems (DBMSs). In many cases, legacy mainframe or midrange systems (IBM or DEC computers) serve as data repositories or servers, with the AIX systems as clients accessing the servers. This case is the *open enterprise computing* model. When PC users enter the picture, the AIX system must serve as an intermediate agent to control PC access to the enterprise. This "three-tiered" architecture — mainframe/server/client — is beyond the scope of basic PC-to-AIX connectivity solutions and will not be covered in this chapter.

If the typical RS/6000 system is a one-person workstation used for scientific or engineering purposes, chances are PC-to-AIX connectivity is not needed. In this case, a package to run Windows applications on the workstation may be desired. These products provide the best of both worlds: the use of personal productivity applications along with powerful UNIX applications on the AIX desktop. A number of commercial products provide this function, but they will not be discussed here.

AIX Connectivity

This chapter will concentrate on PC connectivity to RS/6000 servers, that is, an AIX system that is designed to allow multiple users to connect simultaneously and utilize the resources and services of the system. Methods discussed include terminal emulation, TCP/IP stacks, connectivity for file/printer sharing, integrating AIX with NetWare, and E-mail.

Terminal Emulation

Years ago, multiple users could access UNIX applications from their ASCII terminals. (This is still the case in some UNIX shops.) These applications ran completely on the AIX system and interacted with the user in character mode. Users at their terminals were directly attached to the RS/6000 through an RS-232 connection or remotely attached by modem.

A number of years ago, users began migrating from ASCII terminals to PCs. No longer did they want two "keyboard-and-monitor" sets — one for UNIX applications and one for personal productivity applications — taking up space on their desks. PC users began gaining access to UNIX applications by running terminal emulation software that allowed their PCs to act as "dumb" or ASCII character-based terminals.

In this way, users gained the dual advantages of running Windows personal productivity applications on their PCs while having access to their business-critical UNIX applications. PCs were first connected to the UNIX system over the same RS-232 lines or modem connections that the dumb terminals once used. As more PCs and UNIX systems were connected to LANs, PC users demanded that their terminal emulation programs also run over the Ethernet network.

Terminal emulation programs have evolved significantly over the years. They now contain many connectivity options, emulation types, and networking features. Virtually all terminal emulators support TCP/IP Ethernet connections to the AIX system as well as direct RS-232 and modem connections. All provide popular UNIX terminal emulations such as Wyse 50, Wyse 60, DEC terminals (VT52, VT100, and VT320, for example), and AIXterm. Many emulators can also connect to legacy mainframe and midrange systems, providing IBM 3270 and 5250 emulations. These products are designed to run under Windows, so users can open an AIX session like they would any other Windows application. Depending on the nature of the connection, users can run multiple simultaneous AIX sessions as well. The current emulators can also cut and paste between AIX and Windows applications, run UNIX scripts, record and play back repetitive commands, and much more.

Terminal emulation is the simplest PC-to-AIX connectivity method. Character-based terminal emulation software is inexpensive and runs either over hard-wired RS-232 lines or remotely with a modem. However, such terminal emulation requires the user to have expertise in running AIX applications. In addition, terminal emulation does not give PC users direct access to AIX resources, such as file storage and printer sharing.

The X Window System is a recent improvement over character-based terminal emulation. Its point-and-click graphical user interface (GUI) — similar to Windows or OS/2 GUIs — makes running AIX applications more intuitive. On the PC side, however, users require an X Server software package so that the PC will act as an X terminal when accessing graphical AIX applications. In addition, X terminal emulation packages can be costly, and X applications are typically custom-designed for the particular installation.

Using TCP/IP Stacks

The standard protocol for UNIX communications is TCP/IP over Ethernet. In order to run TCP/IP, the PC requires an Ethernet adapter card and a TCP/IP software package. Ethernet increases communications speed from kilobit speeds to Megabit speeds compared to RS-232. But, more than increasing speed, using TCP/IP protocols lets PC users access networking applications that run over TCP/IP. In particular, a TCP/IP stack is required to run the X Window System and client/server applications such as database management systems (DBMS). TCP/IP is also the protocol used on the Internet. The user gains access to Internet E-mail, the World-Wide Web, and the wealth of other Internet resources.

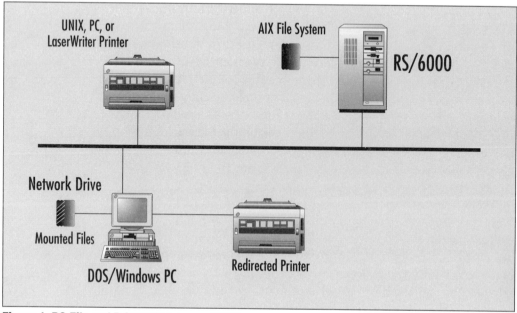

Figure 1. PC File and Printer Sharing on UNIX

Many TCP/IP packages include UNIX-like networking utilities: `telnet`, `ping`, `finger`, the r-commands, etc. Most widely used is file transfer protocol (`ftp`), which allows users to transfer files (a spreadsheet application, for example) from their UNIX systems to their PCs for local processing. Note that file *transfer* differs from file *sharing* (to be discussed later) in that a separate copy of the file resides on the PC and may cause file version control problems.

Drawbacks to running TCP/IP protocols on the PC can include memory usage, cost, and complexity. Some stacks can use up to 250 KB of DOS RAM, but more recent products are DLL- or VxD-based and use up little or no DOS RAM. TCP/IP packages still command a high price point because of the plethora of features included. The cost of the Ethernet adapter must also be considered. Finally, TCP/IP has been difficult to administer, but new utilities such as dynamic host configuration protocol (DHCP) and simple network management protocol (SNMP) are reducing the complexities.

AIX Connectivity for File/Printer Sharing
Potentially, the most valuable use of RS/6000 systems as servers to PCs is in file and printer sharing. PC users benefit from AIX's file storage capabilities. DOS and Windows applications, along with the data used in those PC applications, can now be stored on the RS/6000 server. Once these PC applications and data are on the server, all other PC users can share them. Similarly, when PCs can use printers controlled by the AIX system, the whole organization benefits from sharing printers. Figure 1 diagrams PC file and printer sharing on AIX. Thus, the major benefits of file and printer sharing on AIX include:

◆ Application sharing — PC users can access one network-version copy of the application from the RS/6000 server, reducing administration and easing upgrades.

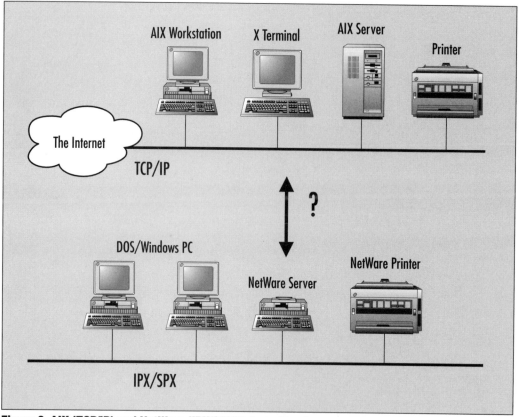

Figure 2. AIX (TCP/IP) and NetWare (IPX/SPX) Integration Issues

◆ File storage — Storing files on the AIX server off-loads the PC's limited disk space.

◆ Printer sharing — Expenses are reduced by spreading the cost of printers over more users.

◆ File/printer sharing — When workgroups can share data, their productivity improves.

Most TCP/IP packages include a Network File System (NFS) client. Originally designed for UNIX workstation networking, NFS is a file sharing protocol that has become a *de facto* standard on virtually all UNIX platforms. NFS was ported to the DOS and Windows operating system to allow PCs to act as NFS client workstations in a network with UNIX servers; the NFS port gave users access to RS/6000 and other NFS servers on the network.

NFS, while ubiquitous in UNIX networking, can be complex to administer. All PC NFS users need to identify each NFS server to which they want access. Identifying the NFS servers is known as designating the NFS "mount points." Each AIX system must also include a table containing the directories available for access by the PC NFS clients as well as the permissions of each user to access those directories. This is known as setting the "NFS exports." With thousands of PCs and dozens (or hundreds) of servers in a large corporate network, these tasks can increase the administrator's burden exponentially.

TCP/IP packages provide shared printer access as well as shared file access. The NFS protocol provides the most common UNIX printer sharing utility, which makes printer access transparent to the user. Another method, the UNIX lpr/lpd protocol, allows PCs to directly access the networked printer.

Another file and printer sharing scheme is based on Server Message Block (SMB) technology, originally developed by Microsoft for serving Windows-based PCs. SMB, often associated with the NetBIOS

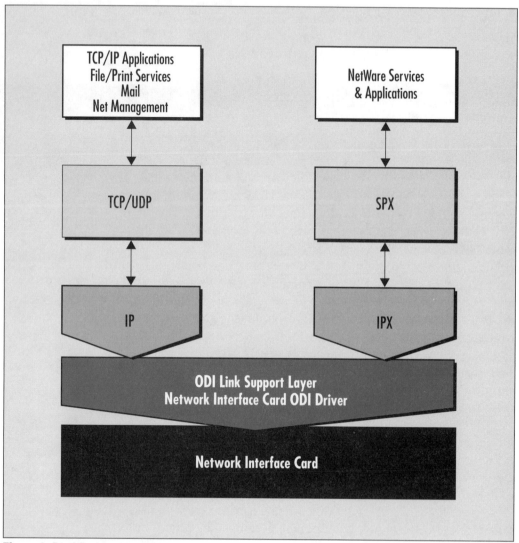

Figure 3. Dual Protocol Architecture

interface and the NetBEUI protocol, is in fact transport independent and can be carried over other protocols such as TCP/IP.

SMB's major advantage is that it runs with off-the-shelf Microsoft clients contained in Windows for Workgroups 3.11 and Windows 95. If used with the NetBEUI protocol, it is limited to operating over a single, bridged LAN network. Alternatively, SMB can run over TCP/IP; however, running SMB over TCP/IP with Windows 3.11 requires a TCP/IP protocol stack. Perhaps the major advantage of using SMB technology, for many AIX system administrators, is that it's available free in Samba, a public-domain SMB implementation.

The major drawback to SMB, since Samba is not a commercial product, is lack of product support from a vendor. On the other hand, some AIX administrators like the fact that it is free and are willing to take on total support responsibility.

Integrating AIX with NetWare

Novell's NetWare is the most popular PC local area networking product, with as much as 65 percent of the market. With NetWare running on a dedicated Intel system, users can share files, applications, and printers running a simple NetWare client on their PCs. NetWare uses a proprietary protocol known as internetwork packet exchange/sequential packet exchange (IPX/SPX) to communicate over Ethernet between NetWare clients and servers.

Although this protocol is optimized for high speed transmission, it is generally limited to the LAN; that is, it does not route well over multiple networks or wide area networks (WANs). On the other hand, TCP/IP is optimized for distributed UNIX file system access, routing data over multiple networks and WANs, and for Internet access. Figure 2 shows the differences in AIX (TCP/IP) and NetWare (IPX/SPX) integration.

As discussed in the previous section, PCs can tap into AIX's inherent file and printer sharing capabilities, allowing the RS/6000 to basically

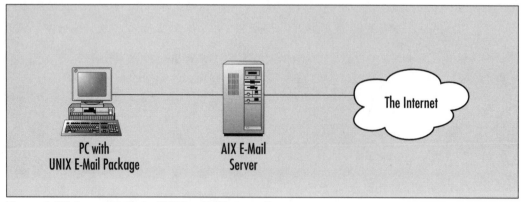

Figure 4. PC Connectivity to AIX E-mail "Gateway"

act like a NetWare server without the need for a dedicated server. However, when there are one or more existing NetWare servers, the solution is to integrate AIX into the NetWare environment. There are several approaches: adding IPX/SPX protocols to the AIX server; adding TCP/IP protocols to the NetWare server; or running dual protocols on the PC.

One approach is to add IPX/SPX protocols to the AIX server. This way, no additional software (TCP/IP) is needed on the PC. The RS/6000 appears as another NetWare server.

Another approach is to add TCP/IP protocols to the NetWare server, thus allowing AIX and PC users who have TCP/IP installed to access the NetWare server.

Both of these approaches add a non-native protocol running on the server, potentially bogging down performance. Another protocol also adds another layer of system administration to the server. In very few cases are AIX administrators trained in NetWare or, conversely, are NetWare administrators familiar with AIX.

As shown in Figure 3, the third approach is to run dual protocols on the PC. Since all Ethernet adapter cards come with ODI drivers, PCs can easily support multiple protocols, thus allowing PCs to access the NetWare server as well as the RS/6000 server, using the protocol native to each server. While this last approach may appear costly in terms of additional software and administration, it is the "wave of the future," giving users all the benefits of NetWare, UNIX, and Internet access while eliminating the foreign-protocol administrative problem. This approach is the one Microsoft used in Windows 95.

Electronic Mail
While not generally included in the realm of AIX connectivity, E-mail is an important consideration in accessing UNIX services from the PC. All RS/6000s contain simple mail transfer protocol (SMTP) and a UNIX mail system. All AIX users have a mailbox from which they can access mail. In fact, AIX systems are very often used

in organizations as an Internet mail "gateway." Figure 4 illustrates this configuration.

PC users can exploit this E-mail gateway by using Windows-based E-mail packages. Post Office Protocol (POP) is an E-mail standard for servers specifically designed to interact with Windows-based E-mail front ends. Depending on the version of the operating system, it may or may not be equipped with POP protocols; if not, the administrator must add POP protocols to the AIX system before it can be used as a mail server and gateway. The Windows E-mail software presents a graphical point-and-click interface to the user. It periodically checks the RS/6000 server for mail on behalf of the user. When mail is present in the user's AIX mailbox, the software transfers it into the PC where it can be read, copied, replied to, or transferred. Most of these UNIX E-mail packages can attach documents to an E-mail message, so that word processing, spreadsheet, or graphics data can be transmitted over the Internet quickly and efficiently to a remote recipient.

A problem may arise when corporations and organizations have already standardized on a PC mail server such as Lotus cc:Mail or Microsoft Mail. Incompatibilities between E-mail packages may arise, but most UNIX E-mail packages handle them effectively.

Windows 95 and Windows NT Clients

Windows 95 and Windows NT go part of the way in addressing multi-platform connectivity. For instance, in Windows 95, Microsoft has included built-in networking capabilities in the "Network Neighbor-hood," a point-and-click graphical browser for accessing files and printers. The decidedly Microsoft approach to networking in Windows 95 and Windows NT makes it easy to connect to other Windows 95, Windows for Workgroups 3.11, and Windows NT systems. However, NetWare and UNIX integration problems still remain. In Windows 95, Microsoft includes a Novell IPX/SPX stack and NetWare client, though recent press reports indicate that there may be some problems using it.

In Windows 95 and Windows NT, Microsoft also includes a 32-bit TCP/IP stack, which provides good UNIX/Internet connectivity and features such as SLIP/PPP. Even though Microsoft has included TCP/IP, they have not included the networking applications that allow access to AIX services.

Microsoft includes only bare-bones `ftp` and `telnet` capabilities. Therefore, if PC users want the benefits of AIX services (file and printer sharing, Windows-based terminal emulation, and so forth), they must add a third-party package compatible with Windows 95 and Windows NT. Many TCP/IP vendors are now offering a 32-bit NFS client and other networking applications to run over Microsoft's TCP/IP.

OS/2 Warp Clients

Many companies, especially those committed to an IBM client/server strategy, are opting for OS/2 Warp because of its built-in business critical features. With OS/2 Warp's true multitasking, multithreading architecture, its crash protection, its memory and data protection features, plus its synergy with Lotus Notes, it is positioned to network with AIX systems for enterprisewide networking.

IBM and third party vendors provide many connectivity options for OS/2 Warp clients, including TCP/IP, NFS client, terminal emulation, and electronic mail. Terminal emulation tends to lean toward the mainframe and midrange environment, with many 3270 and 5150 emulation packages available.

Advanced File Systems and Security

Major advances in UNIX file systems and security have been made in the last few years. These include AFS, Kerberos, and DCE's DFS.

Andrew File System

The Andrew File System (AFS), developed at Carnegie Mellon University, is a distributed network file system for very large enterprises. AFS is now supported as a commercial product by IBM's Transarc Corporation subsidiary.

CONNECTIVITY METHOD	BENEFITS	DRAWBACKS
Character-based terminal emulation	Simple, inexpensive implementation for running UNIX applications from the PC	User must be familiar with UNIX Does not take advantage of other UNIX services (file/printer sharing)
Graphical terminal X emulation (X Windows system)	More intuitive graphical user interface to application	Adds cost for server software on the PC and for X application development
TCP/IP packages	Provide UNIX networking utilities, client/server application support Internet access	Can be expensive Require UNIX knowledge and PC-based administration
NFS client software	Allows UNIX system to act as PC application file and print server Off-loads local PC storage, lets workgroups share applications, printers, and data	Potential for enormous PC client and UNIX server administrative burden in large networks
SMB protocols	Uses existing SMB client software in Windows 3.11 and Windows 95 Available free as public-domain software	NetBEUI protocol limited to local network unless TCP/IP is added Lack of vendor support for freeware version
IPX/SPX protocols on UNIX servers or TCP/IP protocols on NetWare servers	NetWare/UNIX integration without adding software to PC clients	Introduces foreign protocol and additional administrative layer to UNIX and NetWare administration
Dual Protocols on PC (IPX/SPX and TCP/IP)	Standard method for UNIX/NetWare integration Preserves benefits of each protocol	Adds TCP/IP software cost and administration on each PC
UNIX E-mail interface	Use UNIX as E-mail server, Internet mail gateway	Possible incompatibilities with PC-based mail servers
Windows 95 Windows NT	Built-in TCP/IP, IPX/SPX protocols File/printer browsing in "Network Neighborhood"	Lacks UNIX connectivity capabilities Few 32-bit NFS client packages available

Figure 5. Summary of PC-to-UNIX Connectivity Methods

AFS has many advanced features and benefits over NFS:

◆ Appearance of AFS as a single, global file system to the user (Files can reside on many physical servers and over physical WAN links, without users needing to locate them.)

◆ High availability and reliability through file and directory replication and automatic failover

◆ Improved performance through the use of directory caching on the local system

◆ Higher level of security through the Kerberos authentication system and Access Control List (ACL)

Kerberos

Kerberos, developed through MIT's Athena Project, is a highly sophisticated user authentication system that encrypts passwords, employs a single security database, and passes user credentials in the form of "tickets" to access files on multiple systems. Passwords are never passed "in the clear" over the network, thereby reducing the risk of eavesdropping and compromise. Access Control Lists (ACLs) determine which individual users and groups of users can access files and directories through the file system.

DCE's Distributed File System

The successor to AFS — the Distributed File System (DFS) — was chosen as the file system for the Open Software Foundation's (OSF) Distributed Computing Environment (DCE). IBM's Transarc subsidiary supports DFS directly and provides it through OSF to 10 other UNIX vendors. Very similar to AFS in its features and capabilities, DFS uses a newer authentication system (Kerberos version 5) and a more sophisticated ACL paradigm for security. The DCE and its DFS file system have been adopted, or are being pilot tested, by many major corporations and large enterprises throughout the world as the strategic direction for multi-platform computing and application development.

PC Integration

Integrating PCs with AIX systems in an AFS or DFS network may complicate matters. Making the PC a full-blown AFS or DFS client means adding lots of memory and disk space for the DCE runtime libraries and applications, as well as for directory caching. In addition, an AFS or DFS client also needs a powerful Pentium-class processor to perform well.This implementation will usually be limited to newer, more powerful PCs probably running Windows NT.

To integrate the millions of "legacy" 386 and 486 Intel PCs or lower speed Pentium models, a "lightweight" AFS or DFS integration scheme is appropriate. Lightweight technology, as the name implies, does not require adding additional RAM and disk space to the PC. Three lightweight protocols satisfy this scheme:

♦ Use an NFS client and an NFS-to-AFS or NFS-to-DFS gateway on the AIX system. This method works well for organizations that have already standardized on NFS, but is not optimum for performance and security.

♦ Use SMB-based protocols on the AIX system. This approach works well with Windows 3.11 and Windows 95 PCs, but still does not support the Kerberos and ACL security features of AFS and DFS.

♦ Use PC-Interface (PC-I) server on AIX and PC-I client on the PC. Available from PLATINUM technology, this client/server protocol supports both Kerberos and ACL administration.

Summary

Today's users can choose from several approaches to connect PCs to UNIX systems. When choosing a solution, cost and complexity must be taken into account, based on the needs of the organization and the user. Figure 5 summarizes the approaches discussed, along with the benefits and drawbacks of each.

Data Storage and Management

Security Issues:
Comparing RACF to IBM's AIX with Stalker

The ICL Search Accelerator for
The IBM RISC System/6000

HACMP/6000,
the Logical Volume Manager, and Quorum

Stephen E. Smaha
10713 RR 620 North, Suite 521
Austin, Texas 78726

Stephen E. Smaha is president
and founder of Haystack Labs,
Inc. A pioneer in the research and
development of intrusion detection
systems, Smaha has more than
15 years experience in computer
technologies. He has a BA in math
and philosophy from Princeton
University, an MA in philosophy
from the University of Pittsburgh,
and an MS in computer science
from Rutgers University.

Charisse Castagnoli
10713 RR 620 North, Suite 521
Austin, Texas 78726

Charisse Castagnoli is vice president
for business development with
Haystack Labs, Inc. A veteran of
14 years in the computer industry,
Castagnoli worked in software
engineering and management
positions with Texas Instruments,
Teknekron Infoswitch, Convex
Computer, and Secureware, Inc.
She has a bachelor's in computer
science from the University of
California, Berkeley, and holds
a JD from the University of Texas
at Austin.

Jessica Winslow
10713 RR 620 North, Suite 521
Austin, Texas 78726

Jessica Winslow is vice president for
support with Haystack Labs, Inc.
She authored numerous information
resources management policy
publications for the Texas state
government, where she served as
assistant director of a computer
service bureau. Winslow has a
bachelor's degree from Bryn Mawr
College, a master's from Rutgers,
and an MBA from the University
of Texas.

Security Issues: Comparing RACF To IBM's AIX With Stalker

By Stephen E. Smaha, Charisse Castagnoli, and Jessica Winslow

This chapter describes how to configure client/server systems running AIX 4.1 with Stalker* software, a third party package from Haystack Labs, Inc., to implement many of the security and reporting features available in RACF. A feature-by-feature comparison of RACF with AIX running Stalker is included; this comparison should be beneficial to system administrators who are planning to convert from RACF to AIX.

MIS managers and IS personnel are accustomed to the security and reporting features IBM's RACF product provides on mainframe systems. In most cases, these features are required when moving mainframe applications to client/server systems. However, due to differences in operating system design, there is little exact correlation between RACF security features and AIX security features. In particular, AIX provides RACF-style account controls and auditing, but little reporting or verification. When Stalker software is used with AIX, most RACF-style security and reporting features are then available on AIX client/ server systems.

This chapter is organized to follow the six major security areas in RACF, which are:

◆ User Security

◆ Reporting

◆ Resource Control

◆ Auditing

◆ Authorization Checking

◆ Other Security Features

Tables at the end of each section summarize comparisons between RACF and AIX with Stalker. Sample reports show the level of detail available with AIX and Stalker.

This chapter is intended for information systems managers, information technology security managers, security administrators, security analysts, and anyone interested in security on AIX systems.

RACF SECURITY

RACF user security provides the following features:

◆ Requires users to identify and verify their access

◆ Disables access for a particular user (REVOKE)

◆ Restricts access to a machine by time of day

◆ Restricts user access to particular terminals

◆ Generates automatic reports on
   ◇ Failed login events
   ◇ Unauthorized access to resources

Although AIX 4.1 supports many of these features, AIX lacks comprehensive reporting facilities. Stalker's reporting feature supplements AIX to generate RACF-like security precautions and automatic reporting.

User Identification and Authentication

RACF requires users to verify their access to the system, as does AIX. On RACF, a user must be defined in RACF's database, possess a valid password, and in some cases, present a valid group name or operator ID card before gaining access to the system. On AIX, users must have both a valid user name and a valid password. In addition, AIX supports secondary authentication such as smart cards.

Administrators create, delete, and modify user IDs and group IDs in AIX using the System Management Interface Tool (SMIT). AIX supports a number of additional controls over the user password, including restrictions on the characters and words allowed for passwords, minimum and maximum age times, warnings for password expiration, and limitations on password reuse. The SMIT Add User screen controls additional parameters.

AIX permits sharing a single user ID among multiple user names. Although this practice is not recommended, it may be necessary. For example, multiple user names for `root` may exist to avoid sharing the `root` password when multiple individuals have administrative responsibilities. This practice results in an accountability problem, which Stalker software can solve.

AIX tracks and reports activity by audit ID. This is an immutable
ID that is equivalent to the user ID at login. However, when account
sharing is necessary — either to access specific applications or for
administrative purposes — the AIX audit mechanism cannot distinguish between these uses. Stalker creates and manages a session
ID that uncategorically identifies the user login session and thus the
user who originated a particular command.

Stalker also reports on changes to the administrative control files
associated with managing security-relevant aspects of user accounts.
Since the AIX audit mechanism does not report full path names,
without Stalker these types of activities may not be identified. Stalker
generates full path names for all file accesses, including security
administration files.

Disabling a User

In RACF, a user account can be set to the status REVOKED. In this case,
access is denied when the user attempts to log into the account. A
similar capability is available on AIX using SMIT to disable a user
ID by locking the account.

Stalker automatically reports attempts to access locked accounts.
This report shows if an account has been compromised and can
also be an early alert to potential malicious activity by previously
authorized users.

Time of Day Restrictions

One of the parameters in the RACF user profile controls machine access
based on time of day. This parameter is important when the cost of
running a job depends on the time the job is run and when priority
users need greater access.

AIX also supports the time of day feature by restricting users from
logging in during the times specified in the LOGIN TIMES parameter
under SMIT. The login time restrictions are checked only when the
user signs on. Users who exceed their login times are not removed

from the system; therefore, it is important to automatically report any users who exceed their login time limits to ensure that the user account has not been compromised.

Stalker identifies users who exceed their time of day restrictions or attempt to log on outside their allowed login time. A report is automatically sent to the administrator and other managers, if desired.

Terminal Access Restrictions

Reports on actual terminal use are valuable tools for planning and accounting purposes. RACF can restrict system access by terminal id. Terminal access restriction is particularly useful when terminals are located in different physical locations or departments. Terminal access restrictions in AIX using SMIT specify the terminals a user may log in to and use.

If terminal restrictions are in place, it is important to track and report user logins or attempted terminal ID logins. Although AIX does not provide such a utility, Stalker reports on attempts to violate terminal restrictions.

User Authentication

RACF requires users to verify their access to the system, as does AIX. Creation, deletion, and modification of user IDs is done using SMIT. Stalker's added value is its ability to report on all events that modify user IDs or group IDs.

RACF generates user authentication reports through its Login Event Reporting feature. The first of these reports, the password violation report, lists all the password violations for the current reporting session. A second report lists all the failed logons for each user during the reporting session.

While AIX provides limited reporting for user authentication, it does not provide all the relevant information, such as the origination of the logon.

To create a Failed Logon report, use the `auditselect` command to select events from the audit stream. Next, pipe these selected events

```
# /usr/sbin/auditstream | /usr/sbin/auditselect -e "event==USER_Login \
 && result==FAIL" | /usr/sbin/auditpr - t 2 -v >> filename
# cat filename

event        login      status   time                      command
----------   --------   ------   ------------------------   -------
USER_Login   charisse   FAIL     Sun Apr 30 10:39:03 1995   tsm
```

Figure 1. Example of AIX Failed Logon Reporting

```
#
# /usr/sbin/auditstream | /usr/sbin/auditselect -e "event==
 USER_Login \par
 && result== FAIL && time >= 08:00:00 && time <= 17:00:00 && \par
 date >= 04/01/95 && date <= 04/05/95"
 | /usr/sbin/auditpr - t 2 -v >> filename
```

Figure 2. Example of AIX Failed Logon Reporting by Time

through the `auditpr` command, and send the results to a file. (See Figure 1.) If the command appears to hang, it may be a pipe buffering problem. To generate daily or weekly reports, the administrator must manually add time and date selections into the `auditselect` command. Each report must be created individually. (See Figure 2.)

Stalker provides automatic user authentication reporting that handles the pipes, buffers, report formatting, and frequency of background operations. (Reference Figures 3 and 4.) Standard reports include:

◆ Logon and super user activity reports — reports all user logins and superuser access requests

◆ Failed logon report — reports all failed login attempts, the location of the login request (terminal or network ID), and the reason for the login failure

The user security features in AIX are comparable to those in RACF. While AIX alone does not provide the user security reports, AIX with Stalker provides these reports.

RACF RESOURCE CONTROL

RACF provides user-level access control over such general resources as data sets, direct access storage devices (DASD), tape, tape volumes, VM minidisks, terminals, programs, IMS/VS transactions, CICS/VS transactions, and batch jobs. The resources RACF controls depend on the operating system version. For example, IMS and CICS control are available only on mainframes running MVS.

RACF controls access to applications through the general resource profile or the data set profile. General resource profiles specify whether a user or group may access the resource and what the user may do with the resource, such as alter, control (for some specific resources), update, read, execute, and none.

General resource profiles can be applied to resources through the

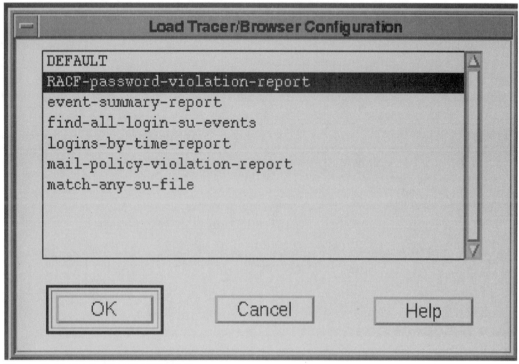

Figure 3. Stalker's Standard Reports

resource naming convention. This practice allows applications to take advantage of a single general profile for all the data sets and program files needed. While AIX does not support general resource profiles *per se*, applications can be arranged in a hierarchy such that group protection can provide a level of security and access control. Stalker supports this use of general resources by providing verification and reporting based on resource naming conventions.

AIX provides an access protection mechanism through group access permissions and Access Control Lists (ACL). ACLs can provide control similar to RACF data set profiles. A substantial difference, however, is that the owner of the resource (the application owner or file owner) controls who may create or change the ACL. Also, ACLs are applied on a file-by-file basis.

In addition to the general resources, RACF provides a mechanism for creating and maintaining group resources by appropriately authorized users.

AIX 4.1 provides some capabilities for managing general resources, as well as a group capability similar to RACF. While AIX does not provide the auditing capabilities by group or resource that RACF provides, AIX with Stalker provides the necessary reports. In addition, Stalker's complete analysis and reporting capabilities allow detailed compliance checks to be applied to most of these resources.

RACF Resources and AIX Features
This section discusses the RACF resources that have parallels in AIX.

DASD — On AIX, DASD systems are hard disks that the logical volume manager (LVM) supports and manages. Only the system administrator has access to LVM. Users cannot create and mount their own DASD volumes. However, the administrator may create network drives that are automatically made available when the user accesses the network drive.

```
-----------------------------------------------------------------------
      "Password Violation Report"
-----------------------------------------------------------------------
Host: vajra    Configuration: RACF-password-violation-report
Date: 08/01/95        Period: 01-Aug-95 12:00:32 -> 01-Aug-95 13:00:14
-----------------------------------------------------------------------

EVENT LOG
TIME                      USERNAME    MECHANISM       SOURCE
-----------------------------------------------------------------------
08/01/95 12:05:02.0       charisse    USER_Login      198.51.46.103
08/01/95 12:08:57.0       snapp       USER_Login      198.51.46.102
08/01/95 12:36:13.0       lalallan    USER_Login
08/01/95 12:45:44.0       root        USER_Login      198.51.46.107
08/01/95 12:57:04.0       snapp       USER_Login      198.51.46.107
-----------------------------------------------------------------------

SUMMARY
USERNAME        MECHANISM        COUNT        SOURCE
-----------------------------------------------------------------------
lalallan        USER_Login       1
snapp           USER_Login       1            198.51.46.102
snapp           USER_Login       1            198.51.46.107
root            USER_Login       1            198.51.46.107
charisse        USER_Login       1            198.51.46.103
-----------------------------------------------------------------------
```

Figure 4. Stalker Login Violation Report

Data Sets — Data Sets on mainframes function like files on AIX. Data Sets can be protected with data set profiles or generic profiles under RACF and protected with group permissions or ACLs under AIX.

Tapes — Under AIX, anyone can read and write to tape devices. Stalker diagnoses whether tape device conflicts are occurring by reporting on tape device accesses and the user IDs accessing tape devices.

Terminals — Under AIX, the "superuser" owns the terminals until a user successfully executes the login process. At that point, terminal ownership changes to the logged-in user. Access from this point on is limited to the logged-in user. The window application aixterm, the general window for typing commands onto an AIX system, is properly configured to the correct ownership. AIX also ships a similar command — xterm — which leaves the window world writable. Thus, aixterm is the preferred terminal window program to use from a security standpoint.

Batch Jobs — AIX supports a batch job facility, at(1), and a time-based job facility, cron(1). The system administrator controls which users can execute batch jobs through either of these facilities. After the administrator enables the batch facility, the user may access it at any time and schedule jobs to run at any time.

General Resources — AIX doesn't report user-based accesses to any of these general resources. Stalker provides detailed reports for any of these types of accesses. Reports can be resource-based, such as "Report all accesses to the tape devices that occurred within a specified time frame," or user-based, such as "Report all accesses by a user to any of the general resources" or "Report all access attempts by non-accounting users to accounting files." Additionally, reports can be limited to only successful accesses or failed accesses.

RACF's Group Mechanism
RACF has a group mechanism, so users can share common resources.

FEATURE		RACF	AIX	AIX + STALKER
Identification & Authentication	Control	Y	Y	Y
	Verify/Report	Y	N	Y
Failed Login Events	Control	Y	Y	Y
	Verify/Report	Y	limited	Y
Disable User	Control	Y	Y	Y
	Verify/Report	Y	N	Y
Time of Day Restrictions	Control	Y	Y	Y
	Verify/Report	Y	N	Y
Terminal Restrictions	Control	Y	Y	Y
	Verify/Report	Y	N	Y

Figure 5. Summary of User Security Features

RESOURCE	RACF	REPORTING	WITH AIX	WITH AIX + STALKER
DASD	profiles	access by user/group	group permissions/ACL	access by user/resource
Data Sets	profiles	access by user/group	group permissions/ACL	access by user/resource
Tapes	profiles	access by user/group	none	access by user/resource
Terminals	profiles	password violation	user configuration	access by user, password violation
Batch Jobs	profiles	access violation	cron/at	access by user/resource
General Resources	profiles	access violations	none	reporting by name type
Groups	profiles	access violations	user configuration	changes to user configurations

Figure 6. Resource Control

All users belong to a primary group and may also belong to other groups. A designated group owner has authority to create data sets and RACF profiles belonging to the group.

AIX also supports a group mechanism comprising resources and users. In AIX, group permissions control access to group-owned resources. Users may enter a new primary group by using the `newgrp` command. AIX also supports a group administration capability. The superuser specifies which user(s) will be the group administrator. This user is now responsible for adding and deleting users from the group. Unfortunately, this feature is difficult to set up and maintain and provides little added administrative benefit. Further, the group administrator must belong to the "security" group, or the SMIT tools will not function properly. Figure 5 summarizes these activities.

Access Control Lists

AIX provides an additional mechanism to control access to individual commands or files, the Access Control List (ACL). ACLs control who can execute programs. The ACL is maintained by the owner of the file, thus administrative responsibility for access to resources controlled by ACLs can be distributed among users. The ACL controls access to the resource at the granularity of a single user. ACLs allow the owner of the file to permit or deny access to the file for single users or groups.

The following command creates an ACL:

```
% acledit filename
```

AIX provides a screen where extended permissions are added. To use ACLs, the "extended permissions" entry in the ACL file must be changed to "enabled." (Further information on ACLs is available in the `man` page on `acledit`.)

Because the AIX audit trail does not report access violations based on group violations or ACL violations, Stalker cannot generate access violation reports based on group or ACL violations. This situation may change in a future AIX release.

FEATURE	RACF	AIX	AIX+STALKER
Command Level Authorization	Y	ACL	Y
General Resource	Y	ACL	Y
Separation of Duties	Y	N	N
Reporting	Y	N	Y

Figure 7. Authorization Checking

```
auditselect -e "Expression"| -f File [Trail]
auditpr [ -m "Message"] [ -t{ 0|1|2}][ -h { elRtcrpP}] [ -r] [ -v]
```

Figure 8. auditselect and auditpr Commands

```
# /usr/sbin/auditstream > /auditfile
# /usr/sbin/auditselect -e "login==charisse && time >=8:00:00 && time <=/
12:00" | auditpr -t 0
```

PROC_Execute	charisse OK	Sun Apr 30 10:38:53 1995 auditselect
PROC_Delete	charisse OK	Sun Apr 30 10:38:53 1995 more
PROC_Delete	charisse OK	Sun Apr 30 10:38:53 1995 bsh
PROC_Create	charisse OK	Sun Apr 30 10:38:53 1995 man
PROC_Execute	charisse OK	Sun Apr 30 10:38:53 1995 bsh
PROC_Create	charisse OK	Sun Apr 30 10:38:53 1995 bsh
PROC_Execute	charisse OK	Sun Apr 30 10:38:53 1995 rm

Figure 9. Reporting on a User's Activities

In general, RACF provides greater control than AIX over resources due, in part, to architectural differences between the two operating systems. UNIX does not support certain mainframe functions, such as the transaction commands Set or Lock Tran, at the operating system level. However, AIX provides several mechanisms for controlling access to resources, such as group access control and ACLs. Since AIX does not provide as much control as RACF, it is critical to verify security integrity by ongoing monitoring and reporting.

The summary chart in Figure 6 shows the resources managed on each system, how access is controlled, and how verification and monitoring are accomplished.

RACF AUTHORIZATION CHECKING

Authorization checking includes the process of granting or denying access to resources and commands based on the user's identity. This section discusses the methods of authorization checking available for RACF and AIX.

General Resources and Commands

RACF checks authorizations in the generic resource profile before users can execute a particular command. The RACF administrator or the delegated security administrator manages user authorization.

AIX does not support this type of authorization mechanism. Instead, AIX controls access to resources and commands at the file level. Either the user group mechanism or individual Access Control Lists manage the authority to execute and access programs.

RACF generates resource authorization violation reports and logs. AIX, although it performs similar checking, does not generate such reports or logs. Additionally, Stalker is not capable of generating these types of reports due to limitations in the AIX audit mechanism. Stalker can report on access or attempted access to various system resources but cannot determine why an access fails.

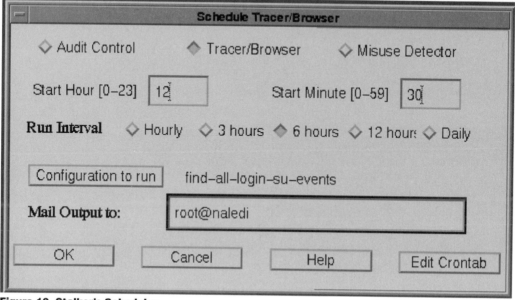

Figure 10. Stalker's Scheduler

Separation of Duties

RACF supports a number of user attributes that allow the user to perform certain functions. Examples of these attributes are ACCT, OPER, and JCL. AIX does not support such user attributes. However, access control to the functions associated with RACF-type user attributes can be controlled using the group or ACL mechanism in AIX.

AIX control using ACLs or groups is less secure because it is more difficult to administer and maintain. The system administrator must create the functional groups and maintain them manually using discrete tools. Since the authorization is based on AIX file permissions, if the owner or permissions of the file inadvertently change, the authorizations may no longer reflect the site's security policy. Further, monitoring authorization grants and denials is limited to the AIX auditing mechanism. In AIX auditing, it is only possible to monitor success or failure — not to determine the cause of the success or failure. (Stalker generates reports that show all access denials a particular user generates.)

However, an AIX utility — `tcbck` — verifies that ownership and permissions on sensitive files have not changed. If permissions have changed, Stalker determines who changed them.

Authorization checking operates on very different models in RACF and AIX; however, it is possible to configure AIX to authorize users for particular resources and commands. To ensure that the appropriate authorizations have been granted, Stalker can be used to report on authorization grants and denials.

RACF REPORTING

RACF generates a number of automatic reports to monitor the security of the system. In addition, RACF's Report Writer allows administrators to create custom reports. AIX has a limited and cumbersome ASCII output generator for audit events. Stalker provides a general purpose audit analysis and report generator for the AIX system.

RACF	STALKER
Select	Tracer/Browser
Date	Time Interval
Events	Event Types
Success	Outcomes
User	Audit User IDs
Nouser	Audit User IDs
Owner	N/A on AIX
Group	Audit User IDs/Group ID
Step	N/A on AIX
Status	Event Types
Process	Event Types
Job	Objects In
Sysid	N/A on AIX
Authority	root or "effective" root
Terminal	Login Source
N/A on RACF	Network ID
N/A on RACF	Misuses

Figure 11. Report Options

General Report Writing

RACF's Report Writer is a text-based reporting tool for creating reports that uses a stream of commands contained in a command file.

AIX provides only a command line utility, called `auditpr`. `auditpr` has over 15 command line options and requires the user to select the audit information with separate commands, `auditstream` or `bincmd` and `auditselect`, as shown in Figure 8.

The example in Figure 9 shows how to use the AIX tools to report on user activities.

Stalker provides a capability similar to RACF's Report Writer, but instead of being command driven, Stalker uses a graphical user interface (GUI) for selecting the relevant information and creating reports. Reports may be automatically run and delivered using electronic mail (E-mail) or sent to a printer or a file. In Stalker, report structures and substructures are stored in an object-oriented database for reuse and retrieval.

As indicated on the screen, administrators can schedule reports to run daily or at other time intervals. Stalker automatically keeps track of which reports to generate and what data needs to be processed.

Predefined Reports

RACF's predefined reports cover the following functions:

◆ Activities

◆ Users

◆ Groups

◆ Resources

◆ Commands

◆ Events

FEATURE	RACF	AIX	AIX + STALKER
Comprehensive Reporting Tool	Y	N	Y w/ Graphical Interface
Standard Reports	Y	N	Y
Customizable Reports	Y	Limited Command Line Only	Y w/ Graphical Interface

Figure 12. Reporting Summary

1. To determine which audit events (from `/etc/security/audit/events`) you wish to edit: edit `/etc/security/audit/config` to select audit events

2. To determine whether you want `bin` collection or `stream` collection: edit the `start` stanza in `/etc/security/audit/config` to enable `bin` collection

3. To set file locations and pre- and post-processing commands: edit the `binmode` stanza in `/etc/security/audit/config` to configure the `bins` and `trail`

4. To specify the post-processing commands (for example, `auditselect`, `auditpr`, or `auditcat`): edit `/etc/security/audit/bincmds`, adding the post-processing

5. To enable auditing, use the command: `# audit start`

Figure 13. Commands for Auditing in AIX

Stalker currently has predefined reports for:

◆ Activities

◆ Users

◆ Resources

◆ Commands

◆ Events

◆ Security violations

The AIX command line tool does not support predefined reports.

Custom Report Writing

In addition to predefined reports, both RACF and Stalker generate user-defined reports. Most of the features in the RACF Report Writer exist in Stalker. Some of the RACF functions are implemented using standard UNIX post-processing tools, such as awk. Figure 11 describes the functions available in Stalker (by menu name) and the associated commands in RACF.

RACF provides a comprehensive reporting tool with the Report Writer program. Stalker provides a graphical selection and reporting tool that enables AIX users to produce comprehensive standard and custom reports with comparable information to the RACF reports, subject to the limitations of AIX.

RACF AUDITING

Auditing is the process by which the system keeps track of user activities. Both RACF and AIX provide auditing systems. The RACF system allows auditing by user and by specific command. The AIX auditing mechanism does not allow auditing on specific commands but by event types and by user. Event types are generally groupings of system level commands, such as file accesses and logons. AIX can also collect site-specific application level events, and Stalker can process these new events like the built-in events.

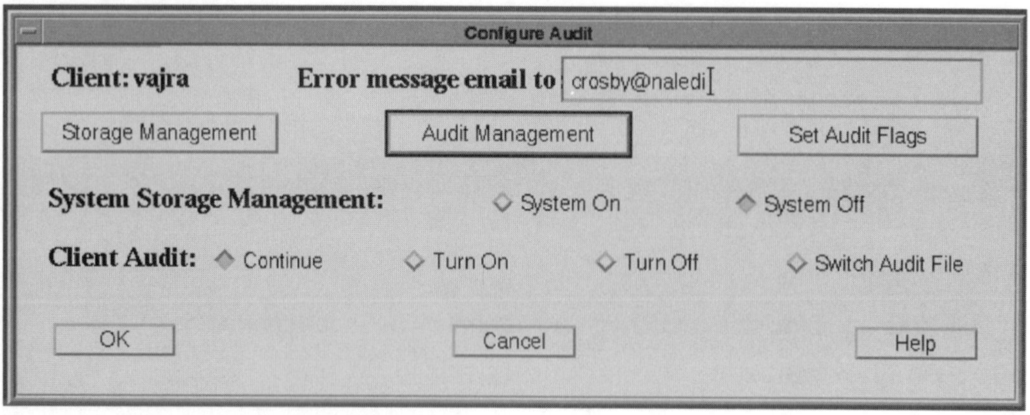

Figure 14. Stalker's Configure Audit Control

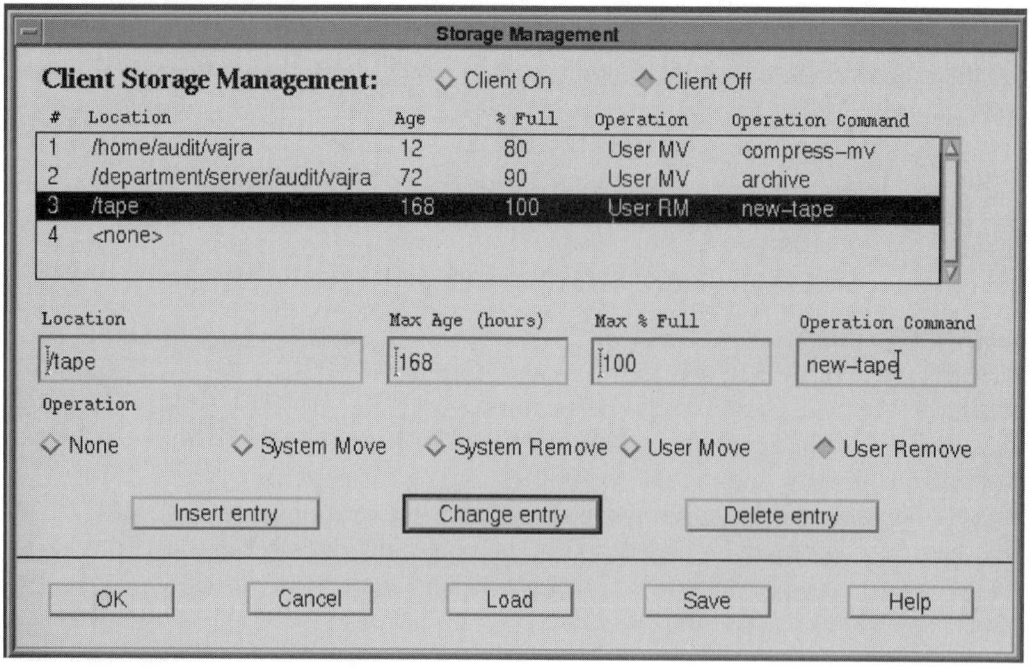

Figure 15. Stalker's Storage Management

Auditing the User

In RACF, the user profile lists the audit events collected for each user. Possible events include administrative activities, access to resources, and access to commands.

AIX provides a graphical interface — SMIT — for setting some user level audit parameters. These events include accesses to security files, user logon events, file access events, and system events such as networking events. Stalker provides a graphical interface to set and manage the user audit attributes and system level audit events.

Enabling Auditing

On RACF, the SETROPTS command enables the collection of specified events for specific users or the whole system. To enable auditing on AIX, several files are edited to configure collection and specify the type, location, and files for audit collection.

Using Stalker, however, audit collection and storage configuration are integrated in the Audit Control module. The configurations are reusable to ensure consistent collection across the network.

Managing Audit Data

The size and growth rate of audit files are functions of the number of events collected. The files can be very large, thus requiring storage management. Because AIX does not provide an audit storage management facility, files must be manually stored and archived. Stalker provides a GUI from which to configure audit storage management and file management by selecting from a number of automatic storage management options, such as move or delete, based on either file size or time. This option minimizes the amount of time spent on managing disk space limitations and archiving.

Both RACF and AIX provide utilities for user audit configuration. AIX tools for audit configuration exist but are cumbersome to use. Stalker provides an integrated user audit configuration and data management facility.

FEATURE	RACF	AIX	AIX+STALKER
User Configuration	Y	Command Line	GUI
Audit Configuration	Y	Command Line	GUI
Audit Data Storage Management	N	N	Y

Figure 16. Auditing Summary

COMPONENT	RACF	AIX
Current System	SYSTEM	uname -a
Group Tree	RACGRP	none
User Attribute	RACUSR	lsuser
Program Properties	SYSPPT	tcbck
System Exits	RACEXT	no equivalent function

Figure 17. System Security Verification Commands

System Verification

RACF and AIX both provide commands that report on the status of
security files and databases on the system. These tools ensure that
important system control files have not been altered and may identify
missing components of user and system security profiles.

RACF

The RACF tool for producing reports on the status of the security
environment is DSMON, which reports on the security status of:

◆ System

◆ Groups

◆ Security properties of programs

◆ User attributes

◆ RACF system procedures and exits

AIX

AIX uses a number of separate tools to generate reports. These reporting
tools are:

tcbck — status of security relevant operating system files

grpck — inconsistency in group database files

usrck — inconsistency in user security files

pwdck — inconsistency in user security files

lsuser — current security information about a user

uname — information about system version (designed to be used by
other commands)

Both RACF and AIX provide tools to verify that the system security
state is consistent. Since RACF maintains separate control information
about resources, it can provide more information than the AIX tools
can. To use all the tools on AIX, in particular tcbck, a user must

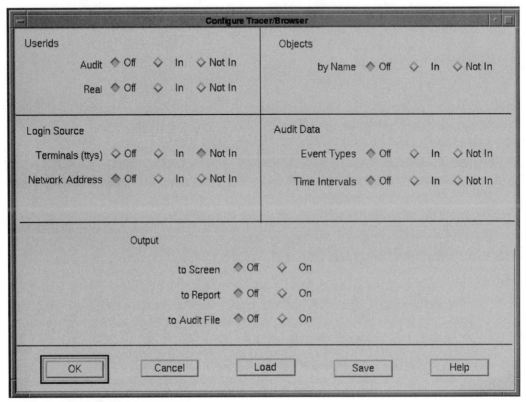

Figure 18. Stalker's Tracer/Browser

install the TCB option on AIX. If this option is not installed, a user must reinstall the operating system to enable use of this feature.

ADDITIONAL FEATURES

The previous sections of this chapter have discussed the features of RACF that are common to AIX and Stalker. This section discusses additional features of Stalker that are not available on RACF due to the differences between mainframe architectures and AIX. Stalker also implements some unique security features that are commercially available only from Haystack Labs.

Networking

On most UNIX systems — including AIX — TCP/IP is the network protocol of choice. Mainframes, however, have adopted TCP/IP at a slower pace; therefore, RACF does not support TCP/IP networking. AIX provides TCP/IP network services such as remote terminal emulation, `telnet` and `rlogin`; file transfer, `FTP` and `rcp`; networked filesystems, NFS; and others.

Network access poses additional security requirements, such as determining who can access the local system using the network and ensuring that only authorized users access network resources. Stalker reports on accesses to the local system by login source or by command. For example, an administrator can use the login source selection criteria to report on all the non-local logins.

An administrator can also report on access to particular networking commands by user or by command. Due to limitations of the NFS protocol, it's not possible for an NFS server to report on client accesses to files that are remotely mounted using NFS. (The clients are responsible for logging those events.)

Misuse Detector

Stalker not only verifies and reports on system activity, but also automatically detects and reports on system security compromise

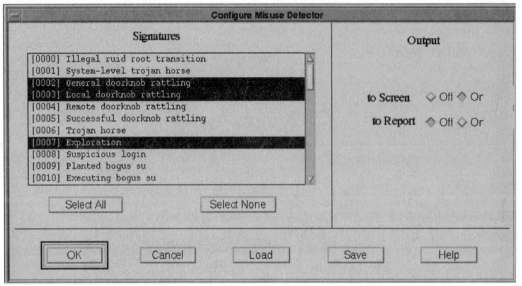

Figure 19. Stalker's Misuse Detector

by outsiders and accidental or intentional misuse by insiders. Using patent pending technology, Stalker's Misuse Detector scans the system audit trail for attack patterns, exploration of system vulnerabilities, and known attack outcomes.

Regular scanning and reporting with the Misuse Detector ensures that the system is not being maliciously attacked or accidentally abused.

Stalker's Misuse Detector detects and reports on system misuse and abuse. Routine reporting minimizes the risk that a system has been compromised or tampered with and provides a history of the system's integrity.

CONCLUSION

Many, but not all, RACF security features have corresponding features on AIX. The combination of AIX and Haystack Labs' Stalker software provides most RACF-style security and reporting features on client/ server systems.

AIX provides the routines and utilities to implement authentication and access control and a limited report writing function. AIX with Stalker provides comprehensive reporting and security tools to implement RACF features, such as the RACF Report Writer and Login Event Reporting. In addition, Stalker monitors network controls and searches for misuse and intrusion.

For more information about Stalker, contact Jessica Winslow at Haystack Labs at (512) 918-3555.

Steve Weeks
IBM UK
1 New Square
Bedfont Lakes
Middlesex, TW14 8HB UK
stevix@uk.ibm.com

Mr. Weeks has worked with IBM's
Unix Systems for 10 years, starting
with PC/IX in 1984. In this time, he
has taught UNIX classes, authored
UNIX books for Addison Wesley,
worked on the UK POSIX Technical
Committee, was technical architect of a
three-tier client/server implementation,
and is currently a principal systems
specialist in IBM UK's National Centre
of Competence.

The ICL Search Accelerator for The IBM RISC System/6000

By Steve Weeks

The ICL Search Accelerator enhances the capability of the RISC System/6000 to support Relational Database Management Systems (RDBMS). This chapter describes the Accelerator and its capabilities, details performance characteristics that the UK's National Centre of Competence observed during technical evaluation, and answers some common questions regarding the Accelerator.

Relational database management systems (RDBMS) make life easier by placing huge amounts of information at a user's fingertips. But, in general, such high-level languages can be a trade-off against efficiency. So many have experienced extended response times while their database retrieves the data of what seems like a simple query.

Furthermore, most enterprises use their databases for multiple purposes. While the main focus of the business may be online transaction processing (OLTP), management often uses the same data for decision-support or online query processing (OLQP). OLTP and OLQP have conflicting requirements. OLTP queries are generally simple, continuous updates to the system. OLQP queries, on the other hand, are sporadic, resource intensive reads from the system. The familiar phrase "full table scan" describes what happens when such large queries cause the system to read an entire table, perhaps to select only a few of a large number of records. The effect on systems activity is twofold:

◆ A full table scan makes the disk very busy, which degrades perceived performance.

◆ Selecting the required rows from the entire table exhausts the entire central processing unit (CPU) resource.

A single MIS inquiry can easily result in 100 percent CPU usage as Figure 1 shows. In such cases, the system is inhospitable to other users while the search takes place.

As a result, the system administrator may want to achieve either or both of two goals:

◆ Improve performance for the OLQP (which is always desirable)

◆ Maintain fast response time for users doing small interactive transactions (which is usually impacted adversely by OLQP)

Normally, the administrator will add indexes to reduce input/output (I/O) and the load on the CPU. However, increased indexing requires additional disk space and increases the amount of time required to update the database tables. Furthermore, indexing does little to improve full table scans.

Fortunately for RISC System/6000 (RS/6000) users, there is another option. International Computers Limited (ICL), a United Kingdom-based supplier of data processing systems and services, developed the ICL Search Accelerator, which offloads database searches from the CPU and provides significant improvements in system throughput and response time. The Accelerator supports Informix Online Version 6, Ingres Release 6.4, and Oracle Version 7.0.16. It works within the database below the structured query language (SQL) interface, so existing applications and data can be used without change.

Understanding the Process

Traditional relational database management systems process queries as shown in Figure 2. Generally, the user submits an SQL statement through the front-end application to the RDBMS server. The server initiates a system call to the AIX operating system, which controls the disks through the small computer system interface (SCSI). The entire table is transferred through the operating system and back to the RDBMS server. The server then selects the "hits" and delivers the correct query result to the front-end application while discarding the rest.

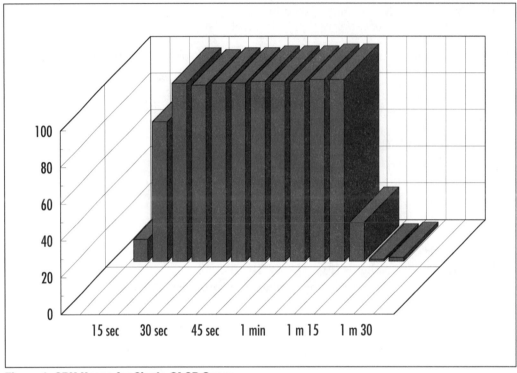

Figure 1. CPU Usage for Single OLQP Query

During this time, AIX uses a lot of CPU to control the disks and transfer the data. Also, the RDBMS uses a lot of CPU to select the wanted records.

How It Works

The ICL Search Accelerator is a separate CPU in a SCSI device that offloads the SCSI controlling work and the record selection process from the RS/6000 CPU. Figure 3 shows how the accelerator accomplishes this process. The SQL query itself is passed directly to the Accelerator. The ICL Search Accelerator hardware initiates SCSI reads, rejects unwanted records, and returns to the RDBMS only the records that satisfy the search specification. As it operates independently of the RS/6000 CPU, it frees the CPU capacity for other work, improving response time on concurrent transactions that can now enjoy substantially reduced CPU utilization.

Installation

During installation, the system administrator links the "Smart Disk Option" to the RDBMS to work with its optimizer. When the RDBMS requests assistance with reading through a large table, the Smart Disk Option sends a message to the ICL Search Accelerator hardware, which is installed in an 8-bit SCSI bus, in place of a SCSI disk. The ICL Search Accelerator is not a Micro Channel Adapter (MCA), but a solid state SCSI device, which can perform very efficient and intensive disk reads. The ICL Search Accelerator performs block transfers of 96 kilobytes (KB), whereas AIX always transfers 4 KB blocks.

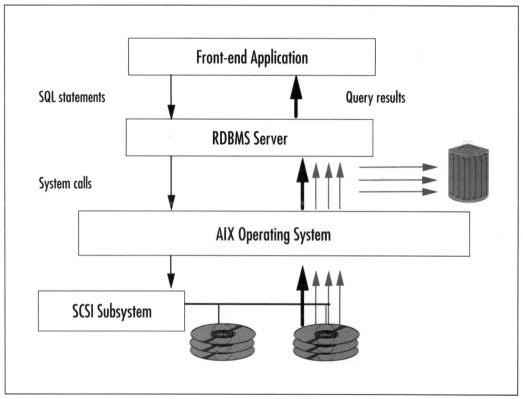

Figure 2. General RDBMS Search Architecture

Putting It to the Test

Most customers want to know not only that a product improves performance, but by how much. Therefore, IBM and ICL put the Accelerator to the test, using a RISC System/6000 Model 590 (66 megahertz Power2 with 512 MB random access memory [RAM]), six 1 GB disks, and AIX 3.2.5 with software fix PTF U434468 addressing a problem in Streams. They used rmss to simulate memory sizes of 64 MB and 192 MB.

Initially, they stored the data on only two disks, as data placement on disks was not considered to be a significant factor in the system performance. For the mixed OLTP/OLQP tests, they moved the single large unindexed table to a third physical disk.

The RDBMS used was Ingres 6.4.03, including the Smart Disk Option. Plans are in the works to repeat the tests with Oracle and Informix, with very similar results expected.

"A/B" testing was easy since the Accelerator can be disabled while the system is running. This feature is not necessarily systemwide but can take effect at the individual user connection to the database.

Measuring Disk Utilization

The AIX performance tools usually provide easy access to accurate measurements of CPU, memory, and disk utilization. However, the ICL Search Accelerator hardware causes some difficulty in disk I/O measurement because it performs I/O without involving AIX. As a result, AIX can report zero percent disk utilization, while the ICL Search Accelerator performs a complete physical scan of a two GB table. During an accelerated scan, AIX can initiate a small amount of I/O and report low data transfer rates with high disk utilization. The systems administrator would have to take the ICL Search Accelerator into account when reading the output of smon, filemon, or

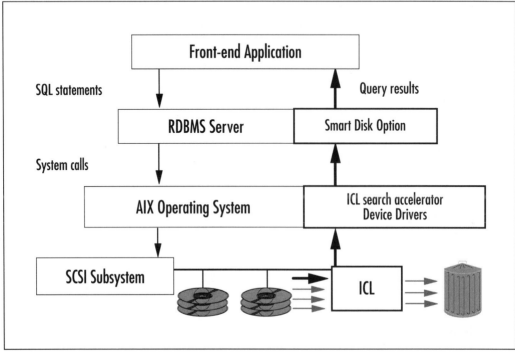

Figure 3. RDBMS Search Architecture with ICL Search Accelerator

`iostat`. These utilities would obtain disk I/O statistics from AIX that are "correct but misleading" while the ICL Search Accelerator is controlling I/O.

The Effect of Adding the ICL Search Accelerator

Figure 4 shows response time increasing with the number of concurrent queries, as one would expect. For one to five queries, the increase is quite linear (top line). In all cases, adding the Accelerator improves the response time by about 60 seconds. IBM and ICL believe the gradient of this slope would be even better if the database were scanning separate tables.

Next, they simulated 192 MB memory instead of 64 MB and switched off the ICL Search Accelerator. The response time improved by only about 34 seconds for a single query, diminishing to an improvement of about 11 seconds for five concurrent queries. The benefit was declining as more queries tried to use the RDBMS cache. The ICL Search Accelerator provides a greater benefit for this specific task, but the option of increased memory might be beneficial to many other types of work.

Single Large Query Analysis

Figure 5 shows an analysis of system activity during execution of a single query. The query was similar to one of the Transaction Processing Council TPC-D transactions and would normally read through a 300 MB table with 1.2 million rows in 128 seconds. This figure shows that the CPU was completely saturated, and disk utilization was about 60 percent. In Figure 6, the ICL Search Accelerator reduces demand for CPU to almost nothing. The graph also shows how AIX reports the disk to be idle when the ICL Search Accelerator hardware was reading actually 96 KB blocks to utilize the disk at 100 percent for the duration of the query.

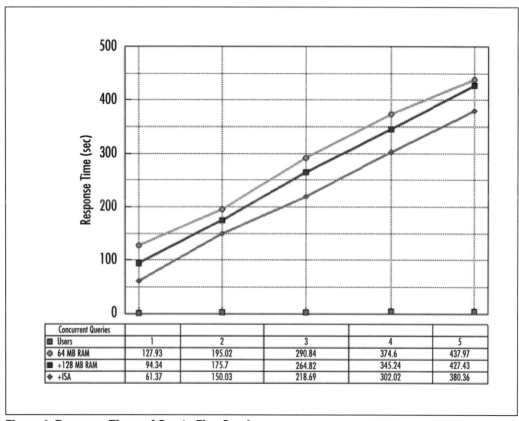

Concurrent Queries					
■ Users	1	2	3	4	5
● 64 MB RAM	127.93	195.02	290.84	374.6	437.97
■ +128 MB RAM	94.34	175.7	264.82	345.24	427.43
◆ +ISA	61.37	150.03	218.69	302.02	380.36

Figure 4. Response Times of One to Five Queries

Concurrent Large Query Analysis

Figure 7 shows two queries executing concurrently. The CPU was once again the bottleneck, running at 100 percent. The disk I/O was spread over a longer period, and disk utilization was lower. Naturally, response time was extended. In Figure 8, the ICL Search Accelerator once again reduces CPU utilization, and again the disk appears to be idle. This pattern was repeated through the series of tests from one to five concurrent queries.

Mixed (OLTP/OLQP) Workloads

As they increased the load from one to five concurrent queries, the CPU never measured more than five percent. The system appeared to have ample CPU capacity to deal with OLTP, but it was anticipated that high disk utilization might extend interactive response times.

Having said this, the ICL Search Accelerator need not be reading all the disks. The system should be able to efficiently perform routine tasks, such as load application code, do paging, and read and write data, provided they are allocated on a different disk from any large tables the ICL Search Accelerator is scanning.

In the final test, they ran two small queries (OLTP) concurrently to simulate a load of just over 100 transactions per minute (tpm). The average response times of the small transactions were 1.7 and 1.8 seconds. They ran them again at the same time as the large, 128-second query. Figure 9 shows the system activity during this test, which ran for 1,742 seconds. The test was then repeated with the ICL Search Accelerator, and the result is shown in Figure 10. The interactive load still makes the CPU very busy, but all response times are substantially improved, as Figure 11 shows. All tests used 192 MB of RAM. The RDBMS was restarted and the memory was flushed between each test.

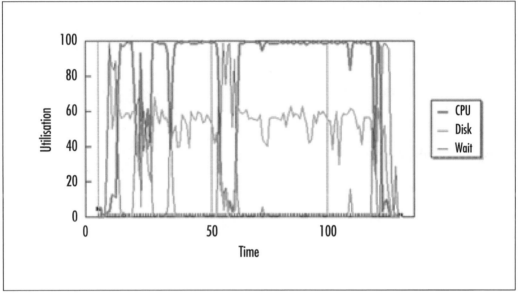

Figure 5. System Activity During Unassisted Single Query

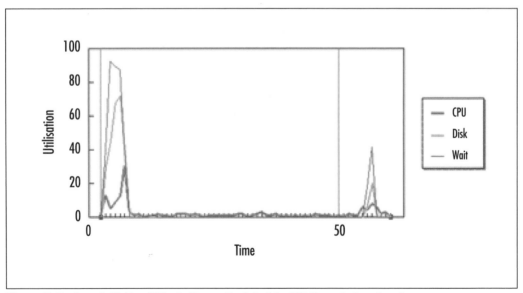

Figure 6. System Activity of Single Query Assisted by ICL Search Accelerator

As the RDBMS tries to share time between large and small queries, the large query response time is extended over 1,000 percent from 128 to 1,742 seconds. The interactive users have their response time extended from 1.7 or 1.8 seconds up to 4.0 or 4.4 seconds (an average over the period).

As the response times show, the ICL Search Accelerator facilitates this mixed workload, keeping the response times down to 1.9 and 2.4 seconds on average for the interactive transactions and 102.8 seconds for the large query.

Testers achieved the results above before placing the data for the OLQP and interactive users on separate disks. The system might have been disk-bound, preventing the interactive users from enjoying the reduction in CPU utilization. Figure 12 shows the response times after separating the OLTP and OLQP work to use separate physical disks.

The Accelerator had, as claimed, enabled the system to sustain good throughput and reduce response times for large queries. Separating the tables to different disks enabled the Accelerator to perform the large query even faster, without impacting the average response time for OLTP.

Frequently Asked Questions
Many users considering installing the ICL Search Accelerator have similar questions. The following are some of the most common questions.

Q: Who needs the Accelerator?
Any user who has large tables and wants to read through them on keys that will not be indexed can benefit from the Accelerator. There are reasons why this can be the case:

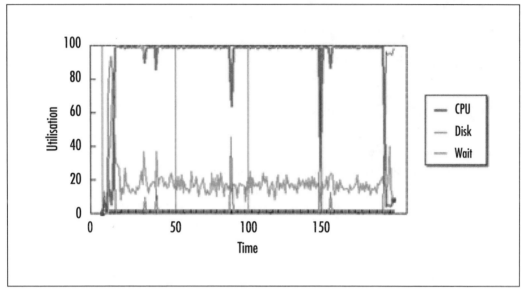

Figure 7. System Activity for Two Unassisted Concurrent Queries

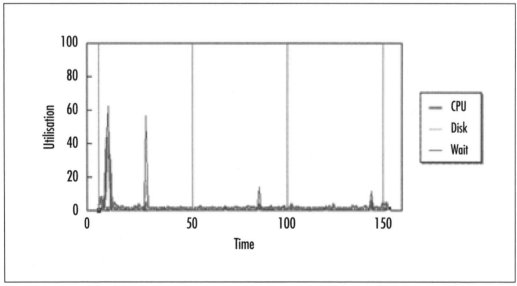

Figure 8. System Activity for Two Concurrent Queries Assisted by ICL Search Accelerator

◆ The key does not help to reduce I/O, *e.g.*, sex (M/F).

◆ The table is highly volatile, and multiple indexes would complicate every update.

◆ The table is often completely refreshed, and multiple indexes would take ages to rebuild.

◆ The unpredictably *ad-hoc* queries would require too many huge indexes.

◆ Searching for sub-strings (`WHERE <field> LIKE %str%`) would always result in a table scan.

Users should note that the break-even point where a scan and an index search take the same elapsed time is about a one percent hit rate (depending on row size, page size, *etc.*) though the scan uses much more processing time. With the ICL Search Accelerator, the break-even point is much lower, approximately 0.3 percent, and the ICL Search Accelerator absorbs the processing cost.

Another benefit is for users who have important data stored in text fields (comments, case notes, details of insurance claims, interviews, modus operandi, delivery instructions). Usually, these data are too unstructured to be reduced to codes for searching. However, the ICL Search Accelerator can allow users to trawl through large amounts of unindexed data without stealing all the CPU from other applications running at the same time.

In such cases, users will need to plan disk usage carefully, as the ICL Search Accelerator will certainly achieve 100 percent utilization of the disk. It may be well for this table to be on a separate SCSI disk and even a separate SCSI adapter if the intention is for other work to continue unaffected by these large queries.

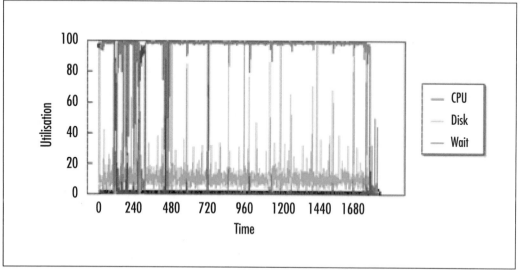

Figure 9. System Activity of Combined One Large Query and Two Small Queries (All OLTP Queries Unassisted by ICL Search Accelerator)

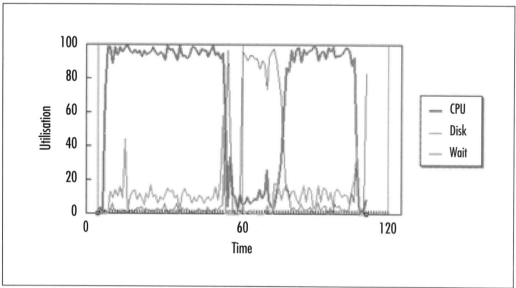

Figure 10. System Activity of Combined One Large Query and Two Small Queries Assisted by ICL Search Accelerator (All OLTP Queries)

Q: Who doesn't need it?

Applications that are principally transaction processing with very localized searching would not be improved. These applications typically have very high volumes of short, updating transactions.

Depending on the balance of the workload, users may, at a similar cost, add 128 MB of memory, which could make a lesser difference to large queries but a positive improvement on many other activities.

Q: How does the ICL Search Accelerator cooperate with RDBMS optimization?

ICL Search Accelerator cooperation optimization actually varies with the RDBMS, but in principle, the RDBMS is able to make cost-based optimizations that take into account the characteristics of the ICL Search Accelerator. When the optimizer is deciding the best way to access a base table, the RDBMS passes the parameters of the search to the Accelerator Library, and the library computes the relative performance of an Accelerator search and a full table scan. The RDBMS then chooses the least cost method (either an index, a table scan, or ICL Search Accelerator search).

Q: How does the ICL Search Accelerator cooperate with RDBMS caching and consistency?

Occasionally, the data on the disk are not in step with the "logical" latest state of the database. To correct this situation, before the ICL Search Accelerator executes the query, the RDBMS forces back to the disk any dirty pages in the "scan area." Different RDBMSs have different ways of providing data consistency, but in all cases, the Accelerator fits into the RDBMS solution. An Accelerator search need not prevent data from being updated on the disk, but the

MEASURED WITH SHARED DISKS	EITHER LARGE QUERY OR OLTP	LARGE QUERY & 100 TPM	LARGE QUERY WITH ACCELERATOR & 100 TPM
Large Query	128 seconds	1742 seconds	102.8 seconds
Small Query 1	1.7 seconds	4.0 seconds	1.9 seconds
Small Query 2	1.8 seconds	4.4 seconds	2.4 seconds

Figure 11. Query Response Times for One Large Query and Two Small Queries Run Concurrently Assisted by ICL Search Accelerator

MEASURED WITH SEPARATE DISKS	EITHER LARGE QUERY OR OLTP	LARGE QUERY & 100 TPM	LARGE QUERY WITH ACCELERATOR & 100 TPM
Large Query	128 seconds	896 seconds	69 seconds
Small Query 1	1.7 seconds	2.2 seconds	2.3 seconds
Small Query 2	1.8 seconds	1.9 seconds	2.0 seconds

Figure 12. ICL Accelerator Assisted Query Response Times After Separating OLQP and Interactive User Data on Different Disks

Accelerator detects both updated data and uncommitted data and invites the RDBMS to search these exception blocks.

Q: What happens when the ICL Search Accelerator and other users access a disk simultaneously?

Other users send their requests to the disk in the usual way, but they get queued when an ICL Search Accelerator transfer is in operation. About every 50 to 100 milliseconds, the disk schedules the non-ICL Search Accelerator work before starting the next ICL Search Accelerator long transfer. If the server has no queued requests, the ICL Search Accelerator can achieve 100 percent utilization of the disk. Administrators will probably need to plan disk usage carefully, as a long accelerator search on one disk will slow throughput of other applications if that disk already has high utilization.

The AIX Logical Volume Manager makes it very easy to spread tables across disks. In this case, a large search will hop from disk to disk instead of monopolizing a single disk for a long time.

Milton H. Edwards
CLAM Associates
101 Main Street
Cambridge, Massachusetts 02142

Milton H. Edwards is a senior technical
writer in the Technical Publications
group at CLAM Associates. Edwards
has a Master's degree in Technical and
Professional Writing from Northeastern
University and is a member of the
Society for Technical Commmunication.

Jim Wentworth
CLAM Associates
101 Main Street
Cambridge, Massachusetts 02142

Jim Wentworth, a support consulting
engineer with CLAM Associates, is
responsible for training programs.
Wentworth has more than 20 years
experience in the computer industry
with operating systems and disk storage
issues. CLAM Associates serves as the
development and level three support
organization for HACMP/6000.

HACMP/6000, the Logical Volume Manager, and Quorum

By Milton H. Edwards and Jim Wentworth

This chapter presents an overview of the quorum feature of the AIX Logical Volume Manager (LVM) and discusses the pros and cons of disabling quorum in HACMP/6000 cluster environments. This information should help system administrators make better informed decisions about quorum issues appropriate for their production environments. The chapter assumes that users understand the AIX Logical Volume Manager and HACMP/6000 concepts and terminology.

High Availability Cluster Multi-Processing/6000 (HACMP/6000) is an IBM offering that enables implementation of a fault resistant application platform. The design of an HACMP/6000 cluster builds upon the robust features of AIX, especially the Journaled File System (JFS) and the Logical Volume Manager (LVM). Quorum is an LVM concept that must be understood and considered when configuring logical volume components in an HACMP/6000 environment. AIX 3.2.3e and later releases now give the option of disabling quorum protection.

WHAT IS QUORUM?

Quorum is a feature of the AIX LVM that determines whether or not a volume group can be placed online, using the `varyonvg` command, and whether or not it can remain online after a failure of one or more of the physical volumes in the volume group.

Volume groups contain two data structures that maintain information about the volume group, as follows:

- The Volume Group Descriptor Area (VGDA) describes the physical volumes (PVs) and logical volumes (LVs) that make up a Volume Group (VG) and maps logical partitions to physical partitions.

- The Volume Group Status Area (VGSA) maintains the status of all physical volumes and physical partitions in the volume group.

To ensure that this mapping and status information accurately reflect the current state of the volume group, VGDA and VGSA data structures are duplicated within a volume group. In a volume group that contains a single physical volume (PV), that physical volume will contain two copies of these structures. In a volume group that contains two physical volumes, the first PV will contain two copies of the VGDA and VGSA; the second PV will contain one copy. In volume groups that contain more than two physical volumes, each PV will contain one copy of the VGDA and VGSA.

VGDA information typically is static, changing only when volume group components are added, modified, or removed. For example, when a logical volume is created or when the size of an existing logical volume is increased, the VGDAs on all physical volumes within a volume group will be updated to reflect the mapping of logical partitions to physical partitions. VGSA information is updated to mark a physical volume as *missing* when it cannot be accessed and to mark a physical partition as *stale* when a write to a physical partition fails.

During normal operations, all copies of the VGDA and VGSA structures within a volume group will be identical. However, if a processor fails before all copies of the VGDA and/or VGSA have been updated, or if a disk drive fails while writing, all copies of the VGDA and VGSA within the volume group may not be the same. LVM uses a *voting* scheme called quorum in which "majority rules" to determine the correct mapping and status information. In reference to a volume group, *quorum* is achieved when more than half of the VGDAs and VGSAs are accessible and identical in content. Having exactly half of the VGDAs and VGSAs accessible and current does not achieve quorum.

WHERE IS QUORUM USED?

Quorum considerations come into play in two ways:

◆ When a volume group is initially brought online using the `varyonvg` command

◆ In determining if a volume group that is currently "varied on" should remain varied on after one or more physical volumes become unavailable because of a failure in a disk subsystem

Quorum at *varyon*

When a volume group is brought online using the `varyonvg` command, VGDA and VGSA data structures are examined. If more than half of the copies are readable and identical in content, quorum is achieved and the `varyonvg` is successful. For example, if one physical volume in a volume group that contains three PVs is inaccessible, the `varyonvg` will be successful because more than half of the VGDAs and VGSAs are still available.

However, if a volume group contains four PVs and two of them are inaccessible, quorum is not achieved **since more than half of the VGDA/VGSAs are not readable**. If a volume group contains two physical volumes and one physical volume fails, the `varyonvg` operation will be successful if the PV that contains two copies of the VGDA and VGSA is still readable and the copies are identical. However, if the PV that contains two copies of the VGDA and VGSA is not readable, quorum is not achieved and the `varyonvg` will fail.

Quorum after *varyon*

If, during normal operations, a write to a physical volume fails, the VGSAs on the other physical volumes within the volume group will be updated to show that this PV has failed. As long as more than half of all VGDAs and VGSAs are writable, quorum is maintained and the volume group remains varied on. If exactly half or less than half of the VGDAs and VGSAs are inaccessible, quorum is lost, the volume group is varied off, and its data become unavailable.

Keep in mind that a volume group can be varied on and/or remain varied on with one or more of the physical volumes unavailable. However, data contained on the missing physical volume obviously will not be accessible. This may not be critical if the data are replicated using LVM mirroring and a mirror copy of the data is still available on another physical volume. Maintaining quorum does not guarantee that all data contained in a volume group are available.

DISABLING QUORUM

AIX 3.2.3e and later versions provide an option to disable quorum checking. With quorum disabled, a volume group will remain varied on until the last physical volume in the volume group becomes unavailable.

An impact of disabling quorum is that, at `varyon` time, all physical volumes must be available and the VGDAs and VGSAs must be current before the volume group will successfully `varyon`. Again, with quorum enabled, only a majority of the physical volumes must be available for `varyonvg` to succeed; but with quorum disabled, all physical volumes in the volume group must be available for the `varyonvg` to be successful.

A volume group with quorum disabled and one or more physical volumes unavailable can be "forced" to `varyon` by using the `-f` flag with the `varyonvg` command. However, forcing a `varyon` with missing disk resources could cause unpredictable results, including a `reducevg` of the physical volume from the volume group. Forcing a `varyon` should be an overt action and should only be performed with a complete understanding of the risks involved.

Quorum checking is enabled by default and can be disabled using either the `chvg -Qn <vgname>` command or the System Management Interface (SMIT) `smit chvg`.

DISK SUBSYSTEM DESIGN GOALS
FOR HIGHLY AVAILABLE SYSTEMS

The goal in designing a highly available system is to ensure that no single failure will result in loss of data or availability of applications. As in designing any system, there will be costs and performance trade-offs. The diagram in Figure 1 summarizes a disk configuration with no single-points-of-failure.

Quorum is not a concern in the configuration shown in Figure 1. Any single failure of a disk drive, adapter, controller, cable, or power source will not result in the loss of quorum and thus the vary off of the volume group and loss of access to data.

WHEN IS IT APPROPRIATE TO DISABLE QUORUM?

Often it is not practical to configure disk resources as shown in Figure 1 because of the expense involved. For example, consider a cluster that requires eight gigabytes (GB) of disk storage (four GB double mirrored). This requirement could be met with two 9333/9334 disk subsystems and two disk adapters in each node. For data availability reasons, logical volumes would be mirrored across disk subsystems. Figure 2 shows such a configuration.

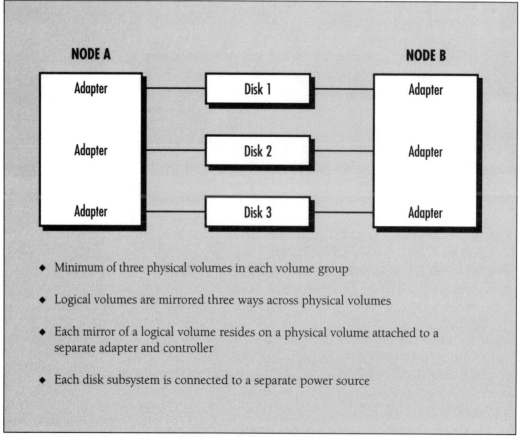

Figure 1. Disk Configuration with No Single-Points-of-Failure

With quorum enabled in the configuration shown in Figure 2, the failure of a single adapter, cable, disk subsystem, or power supply would cause exactly half of the disks to be inaccessible. Quorum would be lost and the volume group varied off, even though a copy of all mirrored logical volumes is still available.

Prior to the availability of AIX 3.2.3e, the only way around this quorum issue was to add a third adapter and another disk to the volume group. This extra disk would not have to contain data but, because it is part of the volume group, it would contain VGDA/VGSA data structures and could be used for quorum determination. This extra disk is referred to as a *quorum buster*. The diagram in Figure 3 shows a configuration with a quorum buster. In this configuration, any single failure — even the failure of a complete disk cabinet — will not result in the loss of quorum and loss of access to mirrored data.

In version 3.2.3e and later releases of AIX, a quorum buster disk is not necessary. The solution is to turn off quorum checking for the volume group. Remember, with quorum disabled, all physical volumes must be available for the `varyonvg` command to be successful.

HACMP/6000 assumes that a volume group is not degraded and all physical volumes are available when the `varyonvg` command is issued at startup or when a volume group resource is taken over during a "fallover." The sample scripts provided with HACMP/6000 do not force `varyon` with the `-f` flag. As stated earlier, forcing a `varyon` could cause unpredictable results. For this reason, modifying the sample script to use the `-f` flag is not recommended. However, with HACMP/6000 version 2.1, it is recommended that a Notify command or Event Recovery command be defined for the `get_disk_vg_fs` sub-event that would alert the system administrator of the `varyonvg` failure and that would require manual intervention to make the volume group resource available.

More advanced Event Recovery commands could be written that would analyze the `varyonvg` failure, evaluate the impact of varying

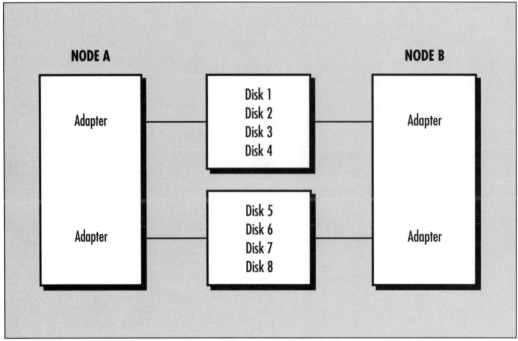

Figure 2. Configuration with Two Disk Subsystems and Two Disk Adapters in Each Node

on the volume group with resources missing, and, if appropriate, force a `varyon`. As always, the Event Recovery command should be tested thoroughly before being applied to a production cluster.

QUORUM CONSIDERATIONS FOR CONCURRENT ACCESS CONFIGURATIONS

With HACMP/6000 concurrent access — Mode 3 — and 9333 disk subsystems, disabling quorum could result in data corruption. For example, consider a cluster with two sets of 9333 subsystems configured for no single point of failure. In this configuration, logical volumes are mirrored across subsystems and each disk subsystem is connected to each node with separate adapters as shown in Figure 4.

If multiple failures cause a loss of communication between node 1 and node 2, both nodes can continue to operate on the same baseline of data from the mirror copy they can access. However, each node will cease to see modifications to data on disk that the other node makes. The result is that the data diverge and become inconsistent between nodes.

On the other hand, if quorum protection is enabled, the communications failure results in one or both nodes varying off the volume group. Although this is a harsh action as far as the application is concerned, data consistency is not compromised.

While this is a specific example, any concurrent access configuration where one or more failures could result in no common shared disk between cluster nodes has the potential for data corruption and/or inconsistency. For this reason, **quorum should NOT be disabled in a HACMP/6000 concurrent access configuration**.

Related to quorum is the "read all copies" option for concurrent access logical volumes. Quorum checking is normally performed when a write operation fails. With the "read all copies" option enabled, all physical volumes that contain mirrors of a logical volume are checked to ensure they are accessible during a read operation. If one or more physical volumes cannot be accessed during a read operation, the physical volumes will be marked as missing and

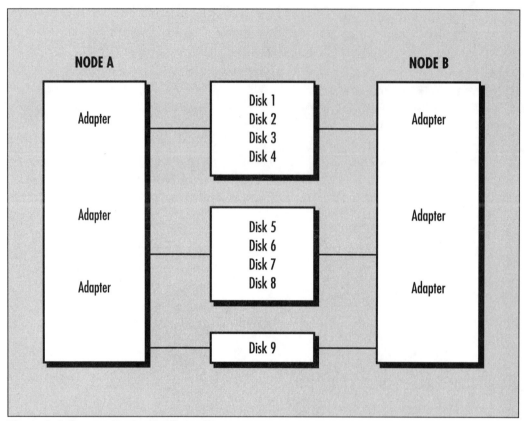

Figure 3. A Quorum Buster Configuration

quorum may or may not result in varying off the volume group. Although there is some overhead associated with the "read all copies" option, the performance impact is minimal. All copies are not actually read; rather, all physical volumes that contain mirrored copies are checked to ensure they are accessible before the read completes. Enabling the "read all copies" option will enable detection during read operations where data contained on mirror copies diverged due to disk failure.

In a concurrent access configuration like that discussed above, consideration should also be given to enabling the "read all copies" option for concurrent access logical volumes. (Refer to the "man page" for the mode3 command for more information about configuring logical volumes with the "read all copies" flag.)

AUGMENTING QUORUM PROTECTION

HACMP/6000 involvement in managing disk resources is limited to varying on volume groups and mounting file systems during cluster startup and failover. The current state of volume group and filesystem resources is not monitored by HACMP/6000; rather, the responsibility is left to the AIX error daemon.

Quorum can actually mask disk subsystem failures. Disk resources can fail and the failure may go undetected as long as quorum is maintained and a good mirror of the data is available. However, the fault "resiliency" of the system could be degraded, as a second failure may result in loss of quorum and the varying off of the volume group.

Although HACMP/6000 does not monitor the status of disk resources, it does provide an easy to use SMIT interface for defining error notification methods. Error notification allows a systems integrator to specify commands to be executed in response to specific errors that are reported to the error daemon. Permanent hardware errors on disk drives, controllers, or adapters may impact the fault resiliency of data. By monitoring these errors through error notification methods, a decision could be made as to the impact of the failure.

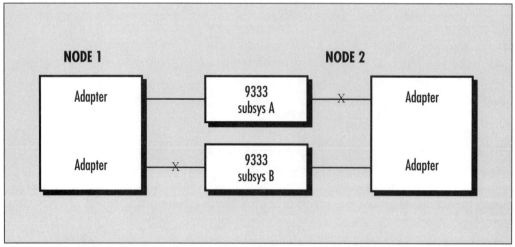

Figure 4. A Two Node Configuration with Two 9333 Subsystems, Configured for No Single Point of Failure

At a minimum, a mail message could be sent to the system administrator to further investigate. A more complex implementation of error notification could include the logic to analyze the failure and make the decision to continue, stop processing, or escalate the failure to a node failure and have the takeover node make the volume group resources available to clients.

It is highly recommended that error notification be implemented for all errors that affect the disk subsystem, regardless of whether quorum is enabled or disabled.

SUMMARY

This chapter discusses the concept of quorum in a AIX environment, explaining when and how it should be enabled when using HACMP/6000 to achieve high availability. Specific scenarios can be constructed where quorum protection does provide some level of protection against data corruption and loss of availability.

In other scenarios, quorum provides no real protection and designing a logical volume configuration for no-single-point-of-failure with quorum enabled may require the purchase of additional hardware.

When planning a high availability configuration, review the implementation plan for the logical volume components carefully. Look at how data availability would be impacted if a disk drive, controller, cable, adapter, or power source fails. And keep the following points in mind as you implement your plan:

◆ Quorum checking is enabled by default and can be disabled with AIX 3.2.3e and later versions.

◆ In non-concurrent access configurations, quorum provides very little actual protection. In fact, enabling quorum may mask failures by allowing a volume group to varyon with missing resources.

◆ Quorum has nothing to do with the availability of mirrored data. It is possible to have a failure(s) that results in loss of all copies of a logical volume, yet the volume group remains varied on since a "quorum" of VGDAs/VGSAs might still be accessible.

- With quorum enabled, more than half of the physical volumes must be available and the VGDA and VGSA data structures must be identical before a volume group can be varied on with the `varyonvg` command. If quorum checking is disabled, all the physical volumes in the volume group must be available and the VGDA data structures must be identical for the `varyonvg` command to succeed.

- A volume group can be "forced" to varyon using the `varyonvg` command with the `-f` flag.

- Quorum should never be disabled in concurrent access configurations since disk subsystem failures could result in nodes accessing diverged database copies.

- Normally, quorum considerations after `varyon` are only invoked during a write operation. The "read all copies" option available for concurrent access logical volumes using LVM will enable quorum detection during reads. This increases data integrity by invoking quorum consideration and varying off a volume group during read operations if no common shared disks are accessible from all nodes. This will prevent an application from reading data that are potentially inconsistent with other mirror copies.

- HACMP/6000 assumes that a volume group is not degraded and all physical volumes that make up the volume group are accessible when a varyon is issued at startup or fallover. The sample scripts provided with HACMP/6000 will fail to varyon a volume group if quorum is disabled and one or more physical volumes in the volume group are unavailable. Customizing the sample scripts to "force" a varyon is not recommended.

- It is highly recommended that error notification be implemented for all errors that affect the disk subsystem, regardless of whether quorum is enabled or disabled. This will ensure that degraded fault resiliency will not go undetected.

Technology Trends

Lotus Notes for AIX:
What It Is and What It Is Not

ATM Performance Analysis:
TURBOWAYS 100 and 155 ATM Adapter
Throughput For Classical IP

Technical Brief:
High Speed Interconnect — Fibre Channel and ATM

64-bit Architectures:
An AIX and RS/6000 Perspective

Technical Brief:
Parallel Computing: Scalability at an Affordable Price

Rufus Woody III
IBM Corporation
One East Kirkwood Boulevard
Roanoke, Texas 76299

Rufus Woody III is a consulting market
support representative on the Lotus
Notes team in IBM's RISC System/6000
Division in Roanoke, TX. Specializing
in the AIX version of Notes, Woody has
supported other AIX-based client/server
offerings in the PC environment. Woody
has supported IBM office systems on
mainframes, minicomputers, and PCs
for more than 15 years. He can be
reached electronically on the Internet
at `aixofc@vnet.ibm.com`.

Lotus Notes For AIX: What It Is and What It Is Not

By Rufus Woody III

Lotus Notes is the industry's leading integrated messaging-based client/server groupware solution. After providing a brief overview of Lotus Notes and some of its new Release 4 features, this chapter discusses why AIX Notes servers may make sense in an environment where increased server capacity is needed or improved administration and management are desired. After listing the software and hardware prerequisites, this chapter provides tips for getting started with Lotus Notes for AIX.

Organizations exploit the power of Lotus Notes — the industry's leading groupware product — to achieve strategic goals quickly and effectively. Notes allows your employees, your customers, and your suppliers to:

◆ Communicate and share key information

◆ Collaborate on projects

◆ Coordinate critical processes

A Lotus Notes for AIX server may make perfect sense in your environment — even if most of your workstations are personal computers. This chapter covers the following topics:

◆ What Lotus Notes is and what it isn't

◆ How Notes provides key solutions to organizations' challenges

◆ What new features are in Notes Release 4

◆ Why you should consider an AIX Notes server

◆ What the software and hardware prerequisites are for Lotus Notes for AIX

◆ How to get started with Lotus Notes for AIX and provide ongoing support

What Is Lotus Notes?

This question is difficult to answer succinctly. Notes is client/server-based and highly scalable. It supports cross-platform clients and servers using a wide variety of communications protocols, including one provided especially for mobile users. And, beginning with Release 4, Notes is fully integrated with the Internet.

Notes provides integrated intra-enterprise and inter-enterprise messaging so that all applications are automatically mail-enabled. It's a distributed *document* database with a powerful replication engine. To help users get started, Notes provides an easy-to-use, integrated application development environment with many samples — whether the job involves custom forms, relational database access, or integration with your favorite desktop products. And, with over 10,000 business partners providing ready-to-use industrial-strength applications, customized application development services, and a wide variety of education and implementation offerings, Notes deployment is easier than ever.

Solutions: Communication, Collaboration, and Coordination

Notes not only lets you communicate within your organization, but also allows you to break through organizational barriers to communicate with customers, business partners, suppliers, support organizations, and regulatory agencies. You may use a variety of electronic mail systems or even the Internet. If you travel, which implies only occasional connection to your primary location, you will enjoy the same degree of communication on a laptop that you do at the office.

Notes goes beyond "just" electronic mail. You can collaborate and share ideas with team members, participate in group discussion forums, post items to or retrieve them from bulletin boards, search distributed document libraries, and access the latest news. You don't have to wait for information to come to you; with Notes, you can find it when you need it.

Notes helps you coordinate critical business processes. With the same infrastructure used for messaging and distributed information sharing, you can use Notes to build custom applications that help you improve customer service, help you get products to market more quickly, make your sales force more effective and more efficient, and help your people be your most valuable asset.

What's New in Lotus Notes Release 4?
Again, this isn't an easy question to answer briefly. However, the improvements generally fall into several broad categories:

♦ Usability

♦ Improved mobile support

♦ Internet integration

♦ Expanded applicaiton development tools

♦ Enhanced administration

♦ Increased performance and scalability

Usability
Release 4 has improved the end user interface (cc:Mail-like three-pane approach, folders, context-sensitive SmartIcons and menus, properties boxes, etc.), added new visual navigators, enhanced editor, improved full text search, simplified creation of user-customizable views, and enhanced personal Name & Address Book.

Improved Mobile Support
With Release 4, you gain improved location support, easier replication, server pass-thru, improved performance through field-level replication, and Help Lite (size and content suitable to laptop usage).

Internet Integration
Notes now offers the integrated InterNotes Web Navigator (with the ability to cache previously browsed pages), InterNotes Web Publisher (which doesn't require end users to know HTML), integrated simple mail transfer protocol mail transfer agent (SMTP MTA), URLs as hot spots in ordinary text, and replication across the Internet.

Expanded Application Development Tools

Also new are LotusScript (a Visual Basic superset enhanced for Notes across all platforms), navigators (graphical access to data), an easy-to-use agent builder, new @Functions and @Commands, new API support, new forms features, improved section support, enhanced table creation, OLE 2.0 support, plus increased practical database size.

Enhanced Administration

Release 4 offers a graphical administration control panel, enhanced control of user roles, integrated Internet offerings, integrated X.400 and SMTP MTAs, pass-thru server support, and Name & Address Book delegation.

Increased Performance and Scalability

Users gain improved overall performance, field-level replication, single copy object store for mail, and exploitation of SMP processors.

While this list is not all-encompassing, it does highlight important improvements to Notes in Release 4.

Lotus Notes for AIX Is Lotus Notes

Almost without exception, Lotus Notes for AIX is *Lotus Notes*. It's still the same client/server-based groupware that leads the industry in helping teams work together better. It still supports PC-based (and other) Notes clients connected over the most popular network protocols to the Notes server — in this case, a Notes server running on AIX, IBM's award-winning UNIX operating system.

Notes Clients

Which clients does Lotus Notes for AIX support? An AIX Notes server can support Lotus Notes clients that are running:

◆ IBM OS/2

◆ Microsoft Windows* (16-bit or 32-bit)

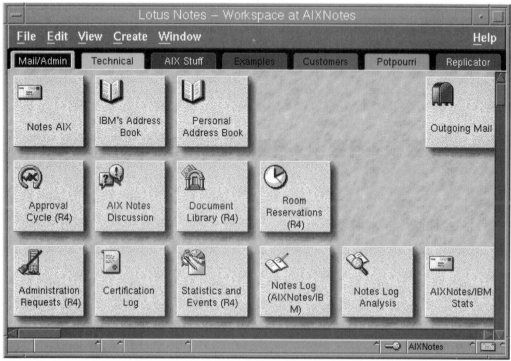

Figure 1. A Lotus Notes for AIX Desktop (Looks just like any other Notes desktop, doesn't it?)

- ◆ IBM AIX (See Figure 1)

- ◆ Other versions of UNIX*, including:
  - ◇ Santa Cruz Operations' SCO ODT*
  - ◇ Hewlett-Packard's HP-UX*
  - ◇ Sun Microsystems' Solaris*

- ◆ Apple Macintosh System 7*

Notes Protocol Support

Which network protocols does Lotus Notes for AIX support? An AIX Notes server can support connections via:

- ◆ Transmission control protocol/Internet protocol (TCP/IP)

- ◆ Novell's sequenced packet exchange (SPX) protocol

- ◆ Notes' X.PC protocol (used by dial-in users)

At UNIX Expo in New York last September, the IBM booth demonstrated connectivity between AIX Notes servers and OS/2 Notes servers, as shown in Figure 2.

Using Release 4's pass-thru server support, Notes clients can connect to or from an AIX server through non-UNIX servers running other protocols. Simply put, clients connecting to a Notes server using protocol A can connect to another Notes server using protocol B as long as the two Notes servers have some protocol in common (among the multiple protocols they may use).

Lotus Notes for AIX In a PC Network

Generally, there are two distinct sets of reasons why you might want to use Lotus Notes for AIX. One obvious reason is when you are using an AIX workstation as a client (an AIX workstation can easily be included in your Notes network). Another common reason to consider an AIX Notes server is that you have a medium-to-large Notes network, and you are concerned with:

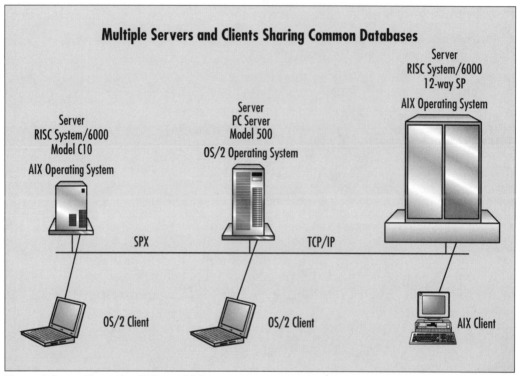

Figure 2. Lotus Notes for AIX and OS/2

◆ Maximum server capacity

◆ A growing systems management (administration) requirement

First, if you have one or more Notes servers, each with a number of users, and second, if you either find response time unacceptable or you can't attain enough throughput for getting the work done in the required time, then you have a "maxed out" Notes server.

If you still have capacity and/or performance challenges — after verifying that you have adequate processor memory and an appropriately configured DASD, and that you have appropriately tuned Notes (including your Notes applications), your operating system, and your network — you might want to consider an AIX server for Notes.

Why should you consider an AIX server for Notes? The answer boils down to four key elements:

◆ The RS/6000's leading-edge RISC-based hardware

◆ The award-winning AIX operating system

◆ A superior SMP architecture

◆ The advantages of the Scalable Parallel (SP) system

The RS/6000 Hardware

AIX runs on the RISC System/6000 (RS/6000), a high-performance RISC-based computer. Some RS/6000s are based on POWER (Performance Optimized With Enhanced RISC) or POWER2 (second-generation POWER) chips. The PowerPC is a newer RISC architecture jointly developed by IBM, Motorola, and Apple Computer. The PowerPC processors being used in the newest RS/6000s demonstrate excellent performance.

The RS/6000 hardware architecture, including its multi-level I/O caching scheme, is known throughout the industry as an excellent performer. Figure 3 shows the broad range of RS/6000 servers

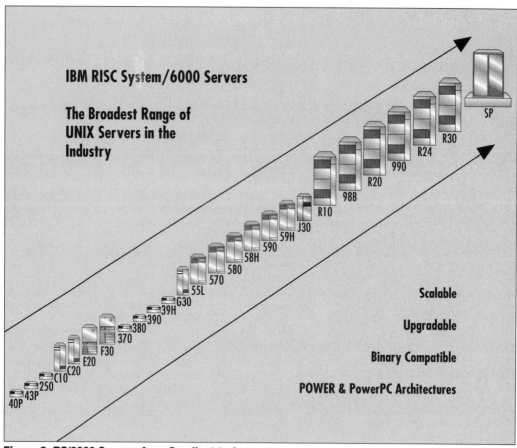

Figure 3. RS/6000 Servers from Smallest to Largest

available. These range from single-engine servers to those supporting SMP to Scalable Parallel systems. SMP and SP are discussed in more detail below.

AIX for Notes System Management and Administration
Operating since 1986 in one of several forms, AIX is IBM's award-winning, high-performance, UNIX-based operating system. AIX's advanced file system architecture delivers excellent performance and reliability. The AIX virtual memory management system is also designed for maximum performance, reliability, and flexibility.

Notes system management and administration are two closely related aspects of the same thing. Of course, administrators have to manage both the servers and the clients. Notes users typically won't see many benefits by consolidating several servers onto fewer AIX Notes servers — unless all users can be consolidated onto one Notes server, thereby eliminating server-to-server replication and server-to-server mail routing. (This consolidation might eliminate using a domain name when mailing, for instance.)

But, as a server or Notes administrator, you may see some benefits if you replace several servers with fewer servers, thereby saving some administrative overhead. It could mean managing fewer system back-ups, doing fewer server logins to administer the network, and having fewer systems on which to install quarterly software upgrades. You'll also have less hardware requiring preventive maintenance, hardware upgrades, uninterruptible power supplies (UPSs), and network and LAN connections.

Two major tools in AIX make it easier to use and easier to manage than other UNIX variants — easier in some cases than PCs. The first tool is the AIX System Management and Installation Tool (SMIT). SMIT is an easy-to-learn, easy-to-use, menu-driven, administrative tool with fast paths for expert users. You can use SMIT to define users, groups, adapters, devices, mountable file systems, directories, system

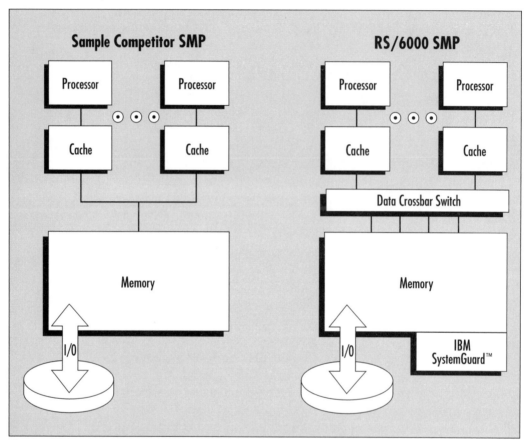

Figure 4. RS/6000 SMP Architecture on AIX Version 4

environments, and network connectivity. You can also perform system
backups or invoke specified DASD backups. Finally, you can use it to
install and maintain IBM system software components.

The second major tool is the award-winning NetView/6000, a
member of IBM's SystemView family of enterprisewide system management products. With fewer servers in your Notes network, alerts
come from fewer nodes, thereby enabling your network support staff
to be more efficient. NetView/6000 is not just limited to managing
AIX workstations attached to an RS/6000; it can also manage PC
clients attached to your AIX Notes server(s) from a single graphical
workstation.

Administration is a tricky subject when limited to Notes administration. Those of you who are or have been Notes administrators know
that Notes administration doesn't mean just waiting to give new Notes
users their ID files. There are databases to manage, servers to certify,
applications to test, security to ensure, systems to back up, and...miles
to go before you sleep.

But with fewer servers to manage, you can pay attention to other
details that get overlooked when you have to manage the server farm
— especially if that server farm has a larger number of nodes than
it should.

SMP on AIX Systems

AIX Version 4 is optimized to support SMP versions of the RS/6000.
RS/6000s in 2-, 4-, 6-, or 8-way configurations — with each engine
having its own cache and with multiple paths to memory through a
sophisticated, high-speed data crossbar switch — to overcome the
bottlenecks inherent in more traditional SMP designs. (For more
details about RS/6000 SMP processors, see the article titled "PowerPC
SMP Servers, Entry Platform Debut" in the January/February 1995
issue of *AIXtra*.) Figure 4 summarizes schematically how SMP works
on an RS/6000 using AIX Version 4.

Beginning with Release 4, Lotus Notes for AIX exploits SMP. Why should you be interested in SMP support? The answer is capacity — more engines to process the same workload means improved scalability and, again, fewer servers to support more users.

Scalable Parallel System

What is a Scalable Parallel (SP) system? (The SP was formerly called the Scalable POWERparallel system, which was shortened to SP2.) It is a unique system in the industry. Think of the SP as a frame with drawers into which you can put specially configured RS/6000 "nodes" connected by a high-speed communications switch and controlled by a single "control workstation." (Note: The SP does not yet support SMP engines, so the current discussion is limited to single-engine nodes.) Several features make the SP powerful, but three apply especially to Notes servers.

First, because the SP is based on the RS/6000 and uses the AIX operating system, all the performance and capacity examples previously discussed apply here.

Second, the high-speed switch is a highly scalable, full-duplex facility for pair-wise communications, operating at up to 40 megabytes (MB) per second in each direction. That is, nodes A1 and A2 can converse at up to 40 MB per second in each direction, for an aggregate communications rate of up to 80 MB per second for that pair. Nodes B1 and B2 can also converse at up to 80 MB per second at the same time. Nodes C1 and C2...you get the picture. What is the limit? For all practical purposes, the limit is the number of nodes in the SP divided by two (to get the number of concurrent pairs).

By bolting frames together, you can currently get a maximum of 512 nodes in one SP. This configuration means up to 256 pairs of nodes and up to 80 MB per second per pair, concurrently. That's power! (Remember, you can start with as few as two nodes and upgrade as your needs change.)

What can you do with the switch? Interactions between Notes clients and servers typically still take place over LAN connections. But what about server-to-server communications? Remember those familiar phrases, "replication" and "mail routing"? If you require multiple nodes, high-speed replication, and/or mail routing in your environment, an SP may help — using the switch — to accomplish this goal efficiently.

Third, the control workstation basically resembles a graphical console from which to manage the SP. It is the way you define your I/O configurations, your networking setup, and your security. It is the way in which you manage backups — even at the node or file level. (Hmmm, all my backups from a single workstation? That sounds convenient!) And, if that same control workstation is your NetView/6000 system management workstation, imagine how — from a single point — you can control your server farm.

SPs can share functions among nodes — some nodes can be AIX Notes servers, while others can run other applications. Lotus Notes for AIX can run on an SP today with Notes Release 4 or Notes Release 3.

Lean and Mean

How does this all net out? The net is that AIX on an RS/6000 uses (in the vernacular) a "lean, mean" operating system running on a "screamer" of a machine.

What does this mean to you? It means that an AIX Notes server, using a RISC-based operating system, can potentially support more Notes clients than another server with a similar CISC-based (*i.e.*, PC-based) configuration. If your PC-based Notes servers are maxed out, then you may want to consider AIX Notes servers instead.

Figure 5 illustrates how CISC-based and RISC-based Notes server capacities overlap and where an SP fits. In Figure 5, note the overlap between high-end CISC servers and low-end RISC servers. Larger RISC-based SMP processors may overlap with lower-end SPs, but

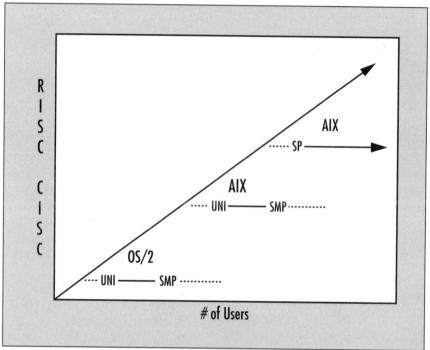

Figure 5. Lotus Notes Server Capacity by Platform

for maximum capacity in a single logical frame, the SP has unique advantages.

There are two subtle aspects of supporting more Notes clients on fewer Notes servers. First, while basic Notes interactive work — clients conversing with servers — is important, so is background work. Therefore, if you have more users per server on fewer servers, you may require less server-to-server replication than you would have with fewer users on a larger number of servers. Second, you may find slightly less external mail routing required if you have twice as many users on a system, since some of the mail is likely to be among users on the same server.

Both of these improvements, though perhaps slight, may decrease the amount of time and network resources required for server-to-server communications. Every CPU cycle saved on background server-to-server tasks can then support interactive Notes client/server functions.

Lotus Notes for AIX Software Prerequisites

Lotus Notes for AIX Release 4 servers, which will support SMP processors, will have AIX 4.1.3+ as a prerequisite. (Lotus Notes for AIX Release 3.x supports uniprocessor mode only and will run on both AIX 3.2.5 and on AIX 4.1.2+.) The Scalable Parallel System (SP) can run Notes Release 4 on AIX 4.1.3+ (or Notes Release 3.x on AIX 3.2.5 or AIX 4.1.2+).

AIX Notes can use TCP/IP, SPX, or X.PC as its communications protocol. You can use just the SPX protocol stack if you need SPX only for Notes support. Or you can use the full NetWare for AIX product if you want this server to be a NetWare server in addition to being a Notes server. Both products are available from IBM.

For more details about the prerequisite program temporary fix (PTF) levels required, contact your Lotus or IBM support channels (see the list at the end of this chapter).

Lotus Notes for AIX Hardware Prerequisites

Lotus Notes for AIX runs on any RISC System/6000 that supports the prerequisite level of AIX, the appropriate memory and DASD requirements, and the physical and protocol connectivity of your choice.

For Release 4, Lotus specifies a minimum of 64 MB of memory and recommends 128 MB. The 128 MB recommendation is preferable, since Lotus Notes for AIX performs better with more memory. In addition, Lotus recommends that you add 16 MB of memory for every 64 users. Typically, users of Lotus Notes for AIX run configurations from 128 MB for smaller systems to 512 MB for extremely large systems.

On AIX, as on other server platforms, Notes performs better with as much DASD as you can afford. The DASD requirement for Lotus Notes for AIX does not significantly differ from that of other platforms. Above the operating-system requirements, Lotus Notes for AIX needs 100 MB for the installation or distribution directory, 20 MB minimum for the server directory (but, more likely, 300 MB for mail and database files), plus expansion based on how much space you require for application data and user mail. If you are going to support a larger number of users, you may end up with a larger DASD configuration than on a non-AIX server; however, since you may also end up with fewer servers, it may be a wash in terms of DASD cost. Still, you should spread Notes application database files and the Notes code libraries across as many high-speed adapters as possible for optimum capacity and performance.

Since Lotus Notes for AIX uses the AIXwindows environment for installation and customization, you will need a graphical workstation for the Notes server. Usually, this workstation is the high function terminal (HFT) used for the system console, but it can be an Xstation if you prefer. Check the Notes documentation for details.

Lotus Notes for AIX comes on an industry-standard CD-ROM, but you may exchange it for an 8 mm tape upon request. Of course, installation via CD-ROM is slightly faster, but, since installation isn't done often, this may be a minor consideration.

Typically, end-user workstations use either token-ring or Ethernet* connections to communicate with the Notes server in the LAN environment. Older RS/6000s come standard with token-ring and Ethernet ports; newer ones come standard with Ethernet ports. (Token-ring support can be added.) Often, traveling users employ asynchronous (TTY) connections and the native Notes X.PC protocol to communicate with the Notes server. All RS/6000s come with some TTY ports. (Additional ports can be added.)

For details about configuring the appropriate hardware, contact your IBM representative or your IBM business partner.

What Lotus Notes for AIX Is Not

Instead of being a matter of what Lotus Notes for AIX isn't, it is really more a matter of what is not yet available.

For example, some communication protocols (*e.g.*, AppleTalk or NetBIOS) may not be supported. As MacTCP's popularity grows, many users are choosing it over AppleTalk. And, as LANs grow, NetBIOS users often are converting to the TCP/IP protocol to avoid the challenges that broadcasts present in an environment with bridges and routers. Plus, with Release 4's pass-thru server support, protocol support should become less of an issue.

Likewise, there may be companion products (*e.g.*, the Notes Fax Server or Lotus Notes Connect for X.25), which are not yet available. You may want to use these companion products on servers that your network outgrew but that still have useful lives as gateways or Notes companion product servers.

Finally, some application development or systems management tools are available only on particular platforms. For example, you may use a tool to develop a Notes client application. If you are not going to run that client application on the Notes server, then it won't matter that this tool is not yet available, unless you also have AIX (or other UNIX) Notes clients that the tool does not yet support. Note that LotusScript is available with Lotus Notes for AIX.

In general, the marketplace tells Lotus in which order to provide companion products, so keep those cards and letters coming, or pass on your requirements to your Lotus or IBM representatives and/or business partners. You may also want to pass your requirements through a user group to which you belong, such as WALNUT (Worldwide Association of Lotus Notes Users of Technology), SHARE (which has an active group of Lotus Notes users), or a local or regional Lotus Notes user group.

Getting Started with Lotus Notes for AIX

Now that you know what Lotus Notes for AIX is and what it isn't, and you've decided to implement an AIX Notes server, what do you do next?

Planning Your Implementation

Ground rule "zero" is to put together an implementation plan. Even though you know how to use Notes, and you may even have some AIX experience, heed the words of the poet Robert Burns, "The best laid schemes o' mice and men gang aft a-gley." I recommend you put together a detailed plan and review it with your Lotus and/or IBM representatives or Lotus/IBM business partner(s). Some of the elements you should include in your plan are discussed here. If you have an existing Notes installation, you should go through the same kind of implementation planning that you would for any new Notes server. Therefore, I'll concentrate on the items that are unique to Lotus Notes for AIX.

Ordering Hardware

If you are not going to use an existing RS/6000, contact your IBM representative or your IBM business partner to order the RS/6000 hardware. You will need to specify which version of AIX to order; I always recommend using the latest level of AIX (currently Version 4), because that version works with Notes Release 4 as well as with Notes Release 3.x. (In fact, although Notes Release 3.33 is the first version to certify support for AIX 4.1.2+, previous releases of Lotus Notes for AIX should work.) Pay attention to the memory and DASD guidelines discussed previously. If you are going to use an existing RS/6000, you will want to do the same planning, but you may not have to order anything other than additional memory and/or DASD and verify that your communications resources (LAN and TTY) are adequate.

Ordering Software

Order Lotus Notes for AIX through your normal channel. As mentioned previously, it comes on CD-ROM, but you can exchange the CD-ROM for an 8 mm tape if you desire. Be sure to order the documentation as well. The installation process is different from that for OS/2, Windows, or NetWare, so you will need documentation.

Installing Lotus Notes for AIX is relatively easy; in fact, novices succeed more often than long-time AIX and UNIX technical staff. Perhaps the reason is that more experienced people may disagree with some of the suggested steps or believe that some don't matter. On the other hand, many installations have succeeded because the naive user followed the directions explicitly, doing simple problem determination/problem source identification (PD/PSI) when things didn't go quite right, and installing all prerequisites, including those that superseded the recommended PTFs.

Providing Technical Support

If you don't have skilled AIX resources in-house, decide where you'll obtain support. You may want to train an employee, hire someone to do the work, or contract with IBM or an IBM business partner. Having skills is desirable, but you may want to use a combination of the above to get started. If you are going to train someone on your staff to support AIX, you should call (800) IBM-TEACh (800-426-8322) to schedule the suggested classes or to order the equivalent computer-based training (CBT) tutorials. Then, see that the training plan is executed appropriately.

Put the appropriate technical support contracts in place. If you already have Notes technical support, this task may be limited to adding AIX support. Since you will need some support on AIX, you might sign up for a level of IBM's AIX Support Family Services. To find out about the available levels of support and consulting, call (800) CALL-AIX (800-225-5249) in the US. (For other countries, contact your IBM representative.)

One option strongly recommended is that you explore TECHLIB. TECHLIB is a compilation of various hints and tips, questions and answers, and maintenance information from IBM's AIX Systems Center in Roanoke, Texas. This information can prove invaluable in various Lotus Notes for AIX situations. To order TECHLIB, call (800) CALL-AIX.

Installing the AIX Notes Server
Finally, you should install or upgrade your hardware. Ensure that AIX is at the proper level, including prerequisite PTFs (see previous comments), and contact your support resources to ensure that you understand the latest details about installing Lotus Notes for AIX.

Do the installation. Test it. Begin coexistence with other servers. Begin migrating users to the new server — and be sure to document what you do along the way, in case you want to save time on the next AIX Notes server you install. This documentation will make system management much easier for your support staff, which in turn makes them more responsive to your users.

Expanding Your Horizons
This chapter intends to convey the following key points:

◆ Lotus Notes, especially with the Release 4 enhancements, is the industry's leading groupware product.

◆ Lotus Notes can enhance the way your organization works with customers, business partners, suppliers, support organizations, and regulatory agencies.

◆ Lotus Notes for AIX is "just" Lotus Notes.

◆ If your Notes server is maxed out, an AIX Notes server may help you by supporting more users per server than other platforms.

◆ There are some minor *caveats*, mostly in terms of companion products (usually gateways or application development tools that may not be supported on all clients or servers).

◆ The range of RS/6000 models — from uniprocessors, to SMP-based models, to the unique Scalable Parallel system — can all support Lotus Notes for AIX.

◆ AIX's excellent implementation of UNIX delivers the appropriate capacity/performance characteristics and system management tools needed in a Notes server environment.

◆ With appropriate planning, configuration, education, and support in place, you can successfully implement Lotus Notes for AIX servers, even in a predominantly PC-based client environment.

If you meet the guidelines discussed above, an AIX Notes server may be appropriate in your Notes network.

Acknowledgments
I thank Bob Mulholland and Bucky Pope of IBM's RISC System/6000 Division, Bob Minns of IBM's Solution Developer Operations, the staff of IBM's Lotus Notes Competency Center, and the staffs of IBM's AIX Systems Center and IBM's Personal Systems Competency Center

Contact phone numbers:

IBM   (800) 547-1283 (IBM's Lotus Notes Competency Center)
                (800) CALL-AIX (IBM's AIX Support Family)

Lotus   (800) 828-7086

SHARE   (312) 822-0932 (ask for the Lotus Notes Project contact)

WALNUT   (508) 475-0729 (World Wide Association of Lotus Notes
                Users of Technology)

for their support and patience during my multi-year learning curve. This chapter would not have been possible without their kind assistance and many spirited discussions. Ed Newberry of IBM's Lotus Brand Management team in Austin, Texas, provided thoughtful insight and some useful graphics for this chapter; his help is greatly appreciated. Finally, I am most grateful for the thoughtful Lotus Notes instruction from my wife, Lisa Woody — she gently and thoroughly ensures that I don't miss some detail that means the difference between success and failure.

Andrew Rindos

Andrew Rindos, who joined IBM in 1988, is currently responsible for end-to-end performance analysis of IBM networking products, including ATM. He holds a BS in zoology, an MS in neurophysiology, and a PhD in electrical engineering (controls) from the University of Maryland. Rindos is adjunct professor at North Carolina State University and Duke University.

Steven Woolet

Steven Woolet, with IBM since 1980, works in ATM software development at Research Triangle Park, NC. Woolet holds a BS in mathematics from Bethel College, IN, a BS in electrical engineering from the University of Notre Dame, an MS in electrical engineering from the University of Minnesota, and a PhD in electrical engineering from Duke University.

David Cosby

David Cosby, with IBM since 1992, develops TURBOWAYS 100 and 155 device drivers for AIX. He works out of IBM's Raleigh, NC site. Cosby holds a BS in both electrical engineering and computer engineering, plus an MS in computer engineering (communications) from North Carolina State University.

Mladen Vouk

Mladen Vouk, currently an associate professor of computer science at North Carolina State University (NCSU) in Raleigh, NC, holds a BS and a PhD from the University of London, UK. Vouk has extensive experience in both commercial software production and academic computing environments. Vouk's work has been supported in part through IBM grants, the IBM-NCSU ATM partnership effort, and a National Science Foundation award.

ATM Performance Analysis:

TURBOWAYS 100 and 155 ATM Adapter Throughput for Classical IP

By Andrew Rindos, Steven Woolet, David Cosby, and Mladen Vouk

This chapter presents direct measurements demonstrating that when the overall ATM environment is properly configured, the TURBOWAYS 100 and 155 ATM adapters can perform close to their designed limits. While the media speed may be 100 or 155 Mbps, several factors — especially workstation configuration and protocol overhead (TCP/IP and ATM) — determine actual throughput of user data.

Throughput measurements using standard industry benchmark applications (including TTCP and Netperf) have shown that the IBM TURBOWAYS 100 and TURBOWAYS 155 ATM adapters perform close to their designed limits if their environments have adequate, properly configured hardware and software. TURBOWAYS 100 and TURBOWAYS 155 adapters support ATM Forum-compliant UNI 3.0 permanent virtual channels (PVCs) and switched virtual channels (SVCs) to operate with similarly compliant switches using ATM Adaptation Layer 5 (AAL 5). This support allows 1024 point-to-point and point-to-multipoint virtual connections. The TURBOWAYS 100 and TURBOWAYS 155's onboard i960 RISC co-processors minimize impact on the RS/6000 processor (CPU).

This chapter discusses AIX-specific host and network parameters that, based on experience, can impact an ATM adapter's performance. When first evaluating ATM technology, most users examine an important Quality of Service (QoS) measurement — throughput.

Factors Influencing Throughput

Throughput can be defined as the amount of data exchanged between systems over a given time interval. In a real production environment, individual components within the larger network can also affect throughput — in fact, the slowest component within a network is the bottleneck that determines that network's maximum throughput.

Since our performance focus was on adapter throughput, we used a very simple test environment with RS/6000s either attached back-to-back (without an ATM switch) or attached to a single ATM switch. Therefore, users planning to implement an ATM environment should remember to factor in potential network delays. Normally, network planners would also need to consider the number of networked users and the impact upon the individual user. This is not a consideration with ATM, however, because it is a switched (not shared) network environment. ATM's QoS plus flow and connection controls provide user bandwidth guarantees.

The following three factors significantly impact overall ATM throughput:

◆ RS/6000 configuration (processor [CPU] speed and operating system)

◆ Upper level protocol effects and overhead (TCP/IP)

◆ ATM protocol overhead (header)

RS/6000 Configuration

The end-to-end throughput that users observe at the application level typically reflects the throughput of the device or process (hardware or software) with the lowest capacity in the path. Such a device or process is referred to as a *bottleneck*. In some cases, especially when multiple resources must be used together at the same time to perform a transaction (such as when a processor simultaneously requires the bus, memory, buffers, etc. to transfer data between two locations), this bottleneck may be quite complex in nature. One possible cause involves queuing delays encountered while gathering the needed resources.

The workstation bus is a typical bottleneck for most communications technologies. ATM 100 or 155 Mbps traffic would pose such a problem for Industry Standard Architecture (ISA) buses in which maximum throughput is about 30 megabytes per second. However, given that the RS/6000 offers either Micro Channel, with a maximum throughput of 40-160 megabytes per second, or Peripheral Component Interconnect (PCI), with a maximum throughput of 132 megabytes per second, neither bus is likely to become a bottleneck unless multiple adapters were installed within a single machine.

More likely, workstation processor speeds will limit system throughput. Generally, less powerful machines cannot deliver data at media speeds. Figure 1 shows the effects of processor speed on TURBOWAYS 100 adapter throughput.

AIX and ATM

Asynchronous transfer mode (ATM) networking is a new international standard for high-speed, cell relay networking. Much of the excitement surrounding ATM stems from its promise of high-speed networking, allowing any mixture of voice, video, and traditional computer data to be transmitted across local, metropolitan/campus, and wide area networks (LANs, MANs, and WANs, respectively).

When IBM introduced its first ATM-compatible product in April 1994 — the TURBOWAYS 100 ATM adapter and device driver for the IBM RISC System/6000 — its driver provided ATM PVC support for transfer control protocol/internet protocol (TCP/IP) as defined in TCP/IP RFC 1577 "Classical IP and ARP Over ATM." Today, this no-charge driver provides ATM PVC and SVC support for Micro Channel RS/6000s running AIX 3.2.5 or AIX 4.1.4. Two connection speeds are available. Users can connect via multi-mode fiber cable to ATM switches at 100 Mbps (sometimes termed "TAXI") or 155 Mbps ("OC3") using the IBM TURBOWAYS 100 or 155 ATM adapter, depending upon their environment. IBM continues to develop new ATM hardware and software for this fast-changing networking environment.

AIX Version 3.2.5	
100 Mbps	PTF U438028
155 Mbps	PTF U440629
AIX Version 4.1.4	
100 Mbps	fileset devices.mca.8f7f
155 Mbps	fileset devices.mca.8f67

In today's businesses, users demand ever higher network throughput for two reasons. First, new applications (video serving, multimedia, real-time video, and collaborative computing) inherently create vast amounts of data requiring increased bandwidth. Second, with the widespread use of PCs and intelligent workstations, the sheer number of networked users can overload traditional LANs and WANs. ATM is designed to provide this high bandwidth, but many users ask, "What type of performance can really be expected?" "What factors limit overall performance?" "What is really practical?" The accompanying chapter adapts AIX-specific information from the "Factors Influencing ATM Adapter Throughput" technical report, available from www.raleigh.ibm.com/tr2/tr2over.html. The technical report addresses ATM adapter performance in IBM's AIX, OS/2, and DOS implementations.

The ATM device driver must compete with other processes (the operating system, protocols, applications, and so forth) for processor cycles. Final throughput depends upon how efficiently the driver and protocol stack utilize the system processor. Figure 2 shows the percent of capacity required by the TURBOWAYS 100 adapter for both AIX ATM device driver versions (3.2.5 and 4.1.4) in tests performed between RS/6000 59H models. Figure 2 also includes the maximum measured throughput numbers for each of the different utilizations. Note: "Netperf" and "TTCP" are special purpose applications used to measure end-to-end throughput.

Processor utilizations less than 100 percent indicate bottlenecks other than the workstation processor. (Workstation processor bottlenecks occur only at the smallest file sizes for the very powerful 59H workstations.) For the data listed in Figure 2, the utilization may appear higher, especially at small file sizes, for AIX Version 4.1.4, compared with AIX Version 3.2.5. However, in these circumstances, throughput generally increases by an even larger factor, indicating greater efficiency in Version 4.1.4's device driver and operating system.

This added efficiency is extremely important to less powerful workstations in which the processor is most likely to become the bottleneck limiting throughput. The dramatic improvements in throughput for small files for the very powerful 59H workstations parallel the dramatic improvements that would be observed across the entire file size range for less powerful machines (*e.g.*, the 520 in Figure 1).

The importance of efficient host processor utilization to throughput becomes even more significant when considering applications that generate the traffic. Since TTCP and Netperf are special purpose applications generating network traffic, a real user environment — potentially running several applications simultaneously — would compete even more for the system processor than these benchmark

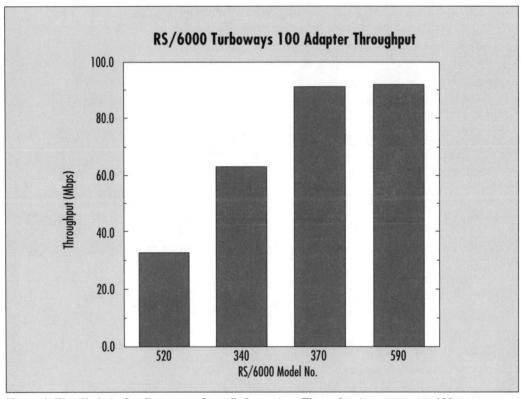

Figure 1. The Workstation Processor Speed's Impact on Throughput — TURBOWAYS 100

applications would. Likewise, within a single machine, host processor efficiency is critical when multiple adapters compete for the system processor.

Upper Level Protocol Overhead (TCP/IP)

Several external mechanisms impact final measured throughput. Among the most important are upper layer protocols such as TCP/IP. Without carefully tuning parameters that control these protocols' behavior, the end-to-end ATM performance may be much less than what the system could otherwise produce.

A protocol's flow control and data recovery methods significantly impact system performance. With IP, for example, TCP attempts to limit data loss and retransmission by using window flow control to manage the maximum amount of outstanding unacknowledged data. Since the window size defines the maximum amount of data transmitted before requiring an acknowledgment of receipt, this paces, and thus potentially limits, the amount of data transmitted. Typically, the larger the window size, the greater the throughput. Unfortunately, since most TCP implementations were originally designed to operate at speeds of less than 10 megabytes per second, TCP flow control mechanisms are not well suited to ATM network speeds. (User datagram protocol [UDP] has no such flow control mechanism.)

Consequently, "TCP Extensions for High Performance" (RFC 1323) were specified for high speed network attachments such as ATM. These extensions provide suggestions for increasing buffering for unacknowledged IP datagrams, the basic message unit in an IP network, (defined by, *e.g.*, `tcp_sendspace` and `tcp_recvspace` for TCP). For peak performance, the sender needs enough buffer space to hold the maximum amount of data sent while the system awaits acknowledgment of receipt from the other end. Buffering must also occur at the receiver to accommodate any differences between the

| FILE SIZE (BYTES) | AIX 3.2.5 | | | AIX 4.1.4 | | |
| | UTILIZATION (%) | | THROUGHPUT | UTILIZATION (%) | | THROUGHPUT |
	(TRANSMIT)	(RECEIVE)	(MBPS)	(TRANSMIT)	(RECEIVE)	(MBPS)
64	100	57	15	96	74	22
128	100	49	23	99	75	40
512	99	46	49	93	61	85
1500	67	60	89	53	40	85
2380	54	55	88	44	35	83
3411	97	54	89	42	34	84
4096	45	51	89	40	33	88
6000	47	51	89	40	32	85
7011	92	50	86	40	33	87
8192	44	50	90	37	32	91
16384	43	50	90	36	32	91

Figure 2. AIX ATM Device Driver Versions 3.2.5 and 4.1.4 — Percentage of Processor Utilization

network delivery rate and the rate at which the system can receive the data and then process it.

TCP `checksum` operations provide reliability but must also compete for the workstation processor. This competition impacts processor utilization as well as overall throughput.

IP typically performs several internal memory-to-memory copies of a given unit of data before moving the data to the adapter for transmission. In one of these intermediate moves under TCP, several datagrams may be concatenated into a single block, up to the maximum transmission unit (MTU) size (when, for example, the data to be sent is smaller than the MTU size). Although concatenation improves the efficiency of moving data across a bus with high transmission overhead (such as Micro Channel), it also introduces storage delays that can impact throughput. In addition, user data larger than the MTU size must be transmitted in two or more datagrams, potentially reducing throughput. This situation explains reduced throughput of files larger than the MTU size for actual data, discussed later in the chapter.

ATM Protocol Overhead (Headers)

The ATM cell format defined by the International Telecommunications Union (ITU), formerly known as the Comité Consultatif International Télègrapique and Télèphonique (CCITT), imposes overhead that impacts information throughput. Five bytes of each 53-byte cell are taken up by the header (control information), leaving 48 bytes for user *payload* (voice, video, or traditional data), which means that only 90.6 percent of the media capacity is available for user information transmission. (A 100 Mbps link is reduced to 90.6 Mbps; a 155.52 Mbps link becomes 140.9 Mbps.)

The user's information is therefore split into 48-byte units (cells) when sent across the ATM network. If any cell ends up with less than

TCP SEND_ & RECV_SPACE (bytes)	TCP THROUGHPUT (Mbps)
16,384	43.9
32,768	71.6
65,536	91.6
524,288	91.7
1,048,576	91.7

Figure 3. Influence of TCP Send/Receive Buffers (8 KB packets)

UDP SEND_ & RECV_SPACE (bytes)	UDP THROUGHPUT (Mbps)
9,216 (Send_Space was 41,600)	91.8
16,384	91.9
32,768	91.5
65,536	92.2

Figure 4. Influence of UDP Send/Receive Buffers (8 KB packets)

48 bytes of user information, the cell will be padded out so that each cell (with header) is exactly 53 bytes long. The payload section of the cell must also carry imbedded header and other overhead information for the higher protocol layers, further reducing the effective amount of user data transmitted.

Other ATM transmission standards may impose additional overhead. The Synchronous Optical NETwork (SONET) 155.52 Mbps physical layer interface defines a 27-cell frame. One cell per 27-cell frame is reserved for control and management, thereby reducing the user payload throughput by another 3.7 percent. This type of fixed overhead most heavily impacts throughput of the smallest length files — the impact is less when all 26 usable cells are filled because the ratio between data and control overhead improves.

TURBOWAYS **Measurements**

This section presents throughput measurements of IBM's AIX implementation of Classical IP over ATM with TURBOWAYS 100 and 155 adapters, as seen by a user whose system resources, in series with the adapters, have adequate capacity and are optimally tuned. **Note:** The datagram throughput obtained is a function of file size, so a given application may not be able to achieve the maximum throughput observed. Throughput will depend upon the mix of datagram sizes the application generates.

User-Level vs. Adapter-Level Throughput

User-level throughput and adapter-level throughput are not the same. *User-level throughput* is the number of data bytes that a user application transmits or receives divided by the time it takes the application to send/receive that data. *Adapter-level throughput* is obtained by correcting the benchmark-generated user-level throughput for protocol and ATM overhead (that is, by adding back to the payload transmitted, the additional ATM and higher layer overhead described above that

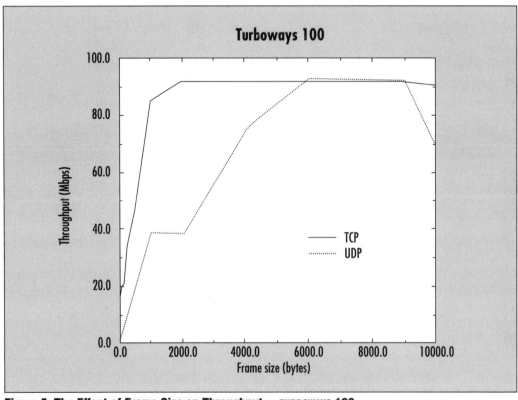

Figure 5. The Effect of Frame Size on Throughput — TURBOWAYS 100

is, in fact, transmitted across the media). Adaptor-level throughput represents an estimate of the actual number of bits per unit time (data plus overhead) that must pass directly through the adapter. Sometimes, adjusting network parameters such as the TCP or UDP send/receive buffer sizes (`sendspace` and `recvspace`) and the MTU size improves the user-level and/or adapter-level throughput.

Effects of Buffer Size on TURBOWAYS 100 Throughput

Figures 3 and 4 summarize TCP and UDP buffer size effects on adapter-level throughput between two IBM RS/6000 model 3BTs with TURBOWAYS 100 adapters connected through an 8260 hub switch. These buffer sizes were manipulated by changing the AIX TCP and UDP `sendspace` and `recvspace` parameters with the `no` (network options) command, which is shell-scripted in the `/etc/rc.net` file. Both `transmit` and `receive` TTCP throughput were measured. Only `receive` throughput is presented, avoiding any "over-reporting" problems commonly attributed to TTCP UDP measurements. (In fact, the UDP receive throughput presented indicates under-reports of actual throughput, as explained below and shown in Figure 6.) The TTCP measurements shown were made using runs of 100,000 eight KB blocks. The default MTU size (9180 bytes) and RFC 1323 (`rfc1323=1` in the `/etc/rc.net` file) were used.

Other combinations of settings (network option parameters) may be needed to maximize the throughput of other specific system and adapter configurations, especially for communicating workstations of unmatched processor speeds. **Note:** For UDP transmissions, changes in `udp_sendspace` and `udp_recvspace` values do not appear to significantly affect throughput.

Effects of File Size on TURBOWAYS 100 Throughput

The TTCP `receive` throughput shown in Figure 5 was measured on IBM RS/6000 Model 3BTs between two TURBOWAYS 100 adapters

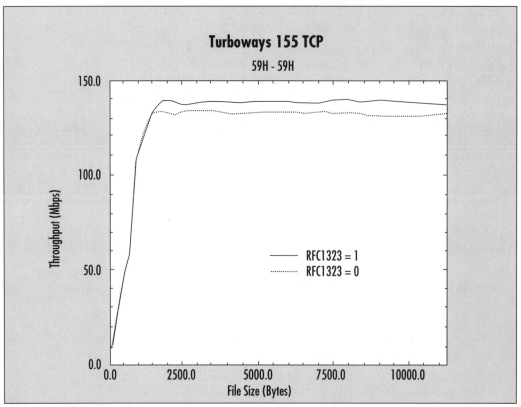

Figure 6. TCP Throughput — TURBOWAYS 155

connected through an 8260 switch. The default MTU size used in these tests, 9,180 bytes, included optimal TCP/IP or UDP/IP parameters, as defined above. The data have been corrected for adapter throughput overhead due to TCP or UDP, IP, and ATM headers.

Figure 5 indicates that TCP performs well across much of the file size range shown, attaining a 92 Mbps maximum throughput. Because data unprotected by flow control and retransmission can be lost, data loss can artificially lower UDP receive throughput. TURBOWAYS 100 is a "deep" adapter, *i.e.*, its i960 co-processor reconstructs the entire frame before passing the frame to the system CPU. As a result, it offloads to the adapter processor work that the host processor would otherwise perform. Losing any single cell within a frame (more likely under UDP) will cause the entire frame to be flushed from the adapter, so that TTCP never sees it at the receiving application layer.

The drop in throughput figures for payloads larger than 9,180 bytes is due to IP fragmentation. Since the MTU size is 9,180 bytes, payloads larger than this must be split into two TCP/IP datagrams. Fragmenting and transmitting these multiple datagrams creates delays and other overhead.

Effects of File Size on TURBOWAYS 155 Throughput

Figure 6 represents measured `receive` throughput (Mbps) versus file size (bytes) obtained with the TTCP test program, the AIX operating system Version 3.2.5, and the TCP/IP protocol. This time, however, files were transmitted between two RS/6000 models 59H connected directly (point-to-point) through TURBOWAYS 155 ATM adapters.

Two RS/6000 model 59Hs were required to drive the adapters at these high speeds. Once again, the default MTU size and the optimal TCP/IP parameters were specified. The data have been corrected for overhead due to SONET, TCP, IP, and ATM headers. The effects of setting the network option parameter `rfc1323` to "on" or "off" are shown. Slightly better performance was observed when `rfc1323 = 1`. The maximum throughput observed was 141 Mbps.

References

◆ Young, Cindy, Tom Adams, and Tim Diefenthaler. */AIXtra: IBM's Magazine For AIX Professionals*, "ATM Networking with AIX on the RISC System/6000," July/August 1994, 36-52.

◆ Young, Cindy, */AIXtra: IBM's Magazine For AIX Professionals*, "Overview of AIX ATM Release 2," July/August 1995, 45-52.

Note: Both of the above ATM articles also appear in the award-winning *The Best of /AIXtra*, Vol. II, Ed., Alan Hodel. Prentice-Hall, 1995.

Technical Brief: High Speed Interconnect — Fibre Channel And ATM

This technical brief discusses some of the key issues surrounding two emerging interconnection technologies, Fibre Channel and Asynchronous Transfer Mode. The intent is to provide an overview of each standard and examine the relationship between the two.

While industry debate continues over which communications technologies will become dominant in the future, two emerging standards-based technologies — Fibre Channel and Asynchronous Transfer Mode (ATM) — will certainly play key roles in the high speed interconnect arena. Fibre Channel and ATM possess unique characteristics that make each desirable for specific application areas, respectively, such as:

Fibre Channel

- ◆ Input/output (I/O)
- ◆ Clustering

Asynchronous Transfer Mode

- ◆ Wide area communications
- ◆ Multimedia applications

Despite some overlap in capability in the local area network (LAN) environment, these two technologies are complementary, rather than mutually exclusive (see Figure 1).

Fibre Channel and ATM each possess unique strengths that reflect the areas of the industry from which they are emerging and the problems they are designed to solve. Both technologies offer unprecedented levels of scalability, flexibility, and performance.

RELATIVE STRENGTHS

Fibre Channel is being developed to resolve fundamental problems related to media dependency, distance, and addressability limitations inherent to traditional channel technologies; doing so extends the benefits of channel technology up into the local area. Fibre Channel provides the kind of fail-safe data transmission controls that channel attached peripheral devices require. ATM is being developed to address problems that are inherent to networks from a networking perspective, such as the seamless integration and management of networks from the local to the global area.

ATM, by pushing wide area network (WAN) communication technology down into the LAN, offers the promise and benefits of a single networking solution from the local to the wide area. Fibre Channel, by combining attributes of both channel and networking technology, brings the concept of "channel networking" and its benefits to reality.

ATM transmission rates scale from 25 megabits (Mbits) per second to 150 Mbits per second today, over unshielded twisted pair wiring, to multi-gigabit rates over fiber optic links in the future, providing a range of options for workstation, server, and backbone connections. These characteristics, coupled with the general acceptance of ATM as the next generation WAN technology of choice, make ATM a natural consideration for high performance, wide area enterprise networks.

Fibre Channel also offers a range of transmission speeds and media options, from 133 Mbits per second over shielded twisted pair wiring to multi-gigabit rates over fiber optic links at distances up to 10 kilometers. Fibre Channel technology also offers the capability to simultaneously carry both channel and network protocols over the same physical media. This capability, coupled with the capability to attach central processing unit (CPU), I/O, and mass storage devices directly to the Fibre Channel fabric — and the ability to address up to 16 million nodes — helps bring new levels of flexibility to users in the local area.

COMPLEMENTARY TECHNOLOGIES

Together, Fibre Channel and ATM technologies can form a foundation for the distributed computing infrastructures of the future. The strengths of both can be applied to the complex and compounding

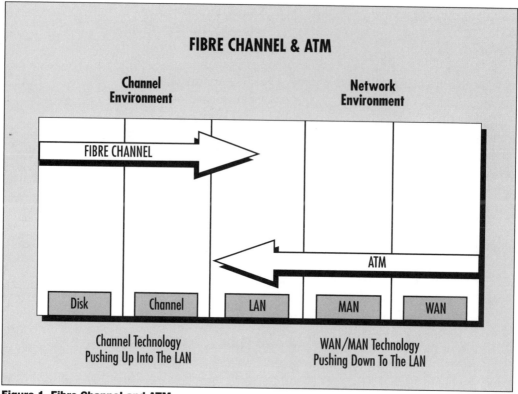

Figure 1. Fibre Channel and ATM

problems of performance, bandwidth, reliability, and management facing information systems and network managers, if Fibre Channel and ATM are viewed as complementary.

IBM endorses both ATM and Fibre Channel technologies and plans to offer solutions in each, while providing an integration of the two where the need exists. For additional information on ATM in the AIX environment, see "ATM Networking With AIX on the RISC System/6000," page 36, */AIXtra: IBM's Magazine For AIX Professionals*, July/August 1994 issue.

Giuseppe G. Facchetti
IBM Corporation
11400 Burnet Road
Austin, Texas 78758
beppe@austin.ibm.com

Facchetti has worked with UNIX systems for 10 years, first with Olivetti in Italy and the U.S. — as a system software engineer. He joined IBM Italy in 1989, working initially as a systems engineer, then as a systems architecture specialist and marketing specialist. He is currently on international assignment to the IBM RISC System/6000 Division in Austin, Texas.

64-bit Architectures: An AIX and RS/6000 Perspective

By Giuseppe G. Facchetti

Rather than describing the PowerPC architecture in detail, this chapter puts 64-bit technology in perspective for business and technical people alike. The chapter reviews the main characteristics of POWER and PowerPC, introduces and describes 64-bit technology, and lists its advantages. The chapter discusses the 64-bit implementations of PowerPC, especially their characteristic aspects, in addition to the support for 64-bit execution. Finally, the chapter describes how AIX is likely to evolve from the current 32-bit support to the new technology, then summarizes the topics discussed.

The definition of the PowerPC architecture derives from the IBM POWER design, in which POWER is an acronym for Performance Optimization With Enhanced RISC. Both POWER and PowerPC are RISC (Reduced Instruction Set Computer) architectures. (IBM Fellow John Cocke first defined the basic principles of RISC architecture in 1974.)

The fundamental characteristics of a RISC architecture are:

◆ **A very *simple architecture* with an *optimized* set of machine instructions**
The instruction set consists only of those elementary operations that the hardware can execute with maximum speed and efficiency. The software generates other, more complex operations by combining several simple machine instructions.

◆ **A very *high instruction execution rate***
The target of RISC architectures is to execute on average about one instruction per machine cycle (faster than traditional architectures, which are typically more complex and therefore slower).

◆ **The fundamental role of *compilers***
The compiler must be able to exploit the hardware architecture by generating instruction sequences that take advantage of the capabilities and performance of the processor.

Although RISC architectures were born as just research projects, in the last several years they have become extremely successful engines of powerful computer systems from both IBM and other vendors. Today, RISC systems (if compared to traditional engines) offer outstanding price/performance ratios, which is one reason they became immediately popular in the UNIX market.

The POWER and PowerPC Architectures
POWER
IBM applied the basic RISC design principles just described, extended

them, and added a number of fundamental architectural enhancements when POWER architecture, along with the IBM RISC System/6000, debuted in 1990.

◆ **Superscalar architecture**
The CPU consists of several specialized units (the first POWER implementation consisted of integer unit, floating-point unit, and branch unit), each dedicated to, and optimized for, a specific function.

◆ **Cache memory**
A cache memory sits between the CPU and main memory. The cache memory is typically divided into two sections, one for data and one for instructions. In this way, for example, while the arithmetic units work on numeric data in the data cache, the branch processor can simultaneously load new instructions from the instruction cache.

◆ **Pipelining**
The CPU executes instructions with a mechanism analogous to an assembly line. Different units of the CPU perform — in parallel — the various operations required for fetching, decoding, and executing instructions. This enhancement allows several instructions to execute at a time — exactly the same way an assembly line works in parallel on many instances of the same product, but at different assembly stages.

Superscalar architecture, cache memory, and pipelining were further extended and optimized in moving from POWER to the POWER2 and PowerPC architectures. In particular, more independent functional units were added, and the function of cache memories and pipelines was improved and made more sophisticated. In addition, PowerPC can also execute in 64-bit mode, which dramatically extends the CPU's capabilities for data handling, memory management, and input/output (I/O) operations.

Microprocessor technology keeps evolving at a fast pace — in performance, miniaturization, and functionality. One of the most interesting changes is the evolution from 32-bit to 64-bit technology, which the PowerPC architecture, along with other industry RISC architectures, supports. This article describes this evolution, delineates some new opportunities for hardware and software developers, and identifies considerations making the technological transition well suited to the IBM RISC System/6000 and the AIX operating system.

These architectural enhancements result in an extremely high level of parallelism in the system. The original *"one instruction per cycle"* target of RISC is overcome: More instructions get loaded in the same cycle (up to four in POWER, up to six in POWER2, and potentially more on PowerPC). This degree of parallelism positions the RS/6000 as one of the most powerful UNIX systems in the industry, with CPUs generally working at substantially lower frequencies than what other RISC architectures require — thus allowing more room for further growth.

PowerPC

The PowerPC architecture was born as part of the agreements that Apple, IBM, and Motorola signed in 1991. These agreements included several joint hardware/software development projects — in particular the PowerPC architecture defined by IBM and Motorola working together at the Somerset Design Center in Austin, Texas.

PowerPC is an *architecture*, not the definition of a particular chip design. The architecture does not even identify a specific CPU block diagram. Only a general model of the logical flow of instructions and data is given, as shown in Figure 1.

The initial plan for PowerPC included four implementations:

◆ The PowerPC 601 processor, currently the engine of several RS/6000 and IBM PowerSeries machine models, as well as a rapidly growing list of systems from other manufacturers, including Apple and Motorola

◆ The PowerPC 603 processor, which addresses the needs of small, low-cost, desktops or portables

◆ The PowerPC 604 processor, aimed at more powerful systems, such as mid- and high-range servers

◆ The PowerPC 620 processor, the first 64-bit implementation of PowerPC architecture, to be the engine of enterprise servers with very high performance and expandability

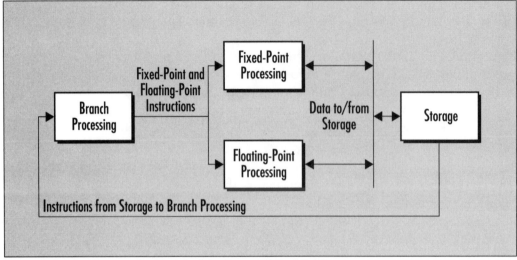

Figure 1. Logical Processing Model of the PowerPC Architecture

ADDRESS LENGTH	FLAT ADDRESS SPACE
8 bit	256 bytes
16 bit	64 kilobytes
32 bit	4 gigabytes
52 bit	4,000 terabytes
64 bit	16,384,000 terabytes

Figure 2. Size of the Address Space Managed by a Processor as a Function of Its Word Length

POWER and PowerPC are completely binary compatible. The main differences between the two architectures can be summarized as follows:

◆ **Single chip implementation**
   PowerPC concentrates all the functional units in a single chip, while POWER was defined as a multi-chip architecture. A single-chip POWER implementation was available on the RS/6000 models 220 and 230. It was called RSC (RISC Single Chip) and was the basis for defining PowerPC.

◆ **Instruction set optimization**
   The PowerPC instruction set has been optimized to have a faster engine. Furthermore, several functions, such as instructions for directly handling single-precision floating-point data, have been added.

◆ **Multiprocessor support**
   PowerPC supports systems based on multiple CPUs, such as symmetric multiprocessors (SMPs). This multiprocessor support allows for memory coherency between the cache memories of the different CPUs to be implemented, as well as supporting all the sophisticated operations required by managing virtual memory in an SMP environment.

◆ **64-bit execution support**
   The PowerPC architecture includes instructions that handle 64-bit long data and addresses.

What 64-bit Architecture Means

Although the vast majority of current applications do not need the functions and capabilities of a 64-bit architecture, the applications of the near future will more and more view 32-bit technology as a limiting factor. In fact, examples of environments requiring large memories and large files already exist.

For example, some artificial intelligence programs that control
either the function of complex industrial processes or the behavior
of human beings in critical operations (aircraft control, for example)
"learn" from experience and grow to huge sizes. In addition, imaging
applications, such as graphics document retrieval systems for public
administration or police work, require very large files in order to store
scanned documents or pictures.

These examples show that the ability to manage larger programs
and data is going to be very important in the future, and that 64-bit
architectures should play a key role in this evolution. However,
before different hardware vendors begin developing their own ideas
of what 64-bit systems should look like and how they should behave,
it is vital that the industry defines and agrees upon standards. Otherwise, the resulting software incompatibilities would soon impact
both customers' and software providers' ability to choose the system
platform that best suits their needs or to easily move applications
between platforms.

In a cooperative effort, the most important UNIX hardware vendors
ratified an initiative on 64-bit computing. Information on this initiative
appears at the end of this chapter.

64-bit Addresses and
64-bit Arithmetic

In defining 64-bit architecture from an operational standpoint, the
following criteria apply:

♦ 64-bit architecture can handle 64-bit long data; in other words, a
contiguous block of 64 bits (8 bytes) in memory is defined as one
of the elementary units that the CPU can handle. This means that
the instruction set includes instructions for moving a 64-bit long
datum, as well as arithmetic instructions for performing arithmetic
operations on 64-bit long integers.

◆ 64-bit architecture generates 64-bit long addresses, both as *effective addresses* (the addresses generated and utilized by machine instructions) and as *physical addresses* (those that address the memory cards plugged into the machine memory slots). Individual processor implementations may generate shorter physical addresses, but the architecture must support up to 64-bit long ones.

The two great advantages of a 64-bit architecture, therefore, are its ability to use very long integers in computation and its ability to address huge address spaces. Using very long integers for computation can be very useful in specialized applications, in addition to managing very large file systems. The ability to address huge address spaces, both in virtual and physical memory, can be exploited by all those applications that need to access very large amounts of data, such as massive databases or imaging applications.

Addressability is the more important aspect, as we expect that future, complex applications (large databases, large numeric applications, and multimedia environments) will need to manage and operate on larger and larger data sets. Figure 2 shows the size of the address spaces that can be managed as a function of the length of the address that the CPU generates. A 64-bit architecture can address a huge address space.

One goal of the 64-bit version of PowerPC is to maintain binary compatibility with the current PowerPC processors. From the standpoint of the 32-bit and 64-bit specifications, there are a few differences, as shown in Figure 3. The number of CPU registers (the basic storage cell where the CPU stores the data on which it performs its computations) remains the same, but these registers are 64 bits long instead of 32 bits long. A few other control registers move from 32 to 64 bits in length. As shown, floating-point registers do not change in size, as they conform to industry standards for floating-points, which require 32- or 64-bit long data.

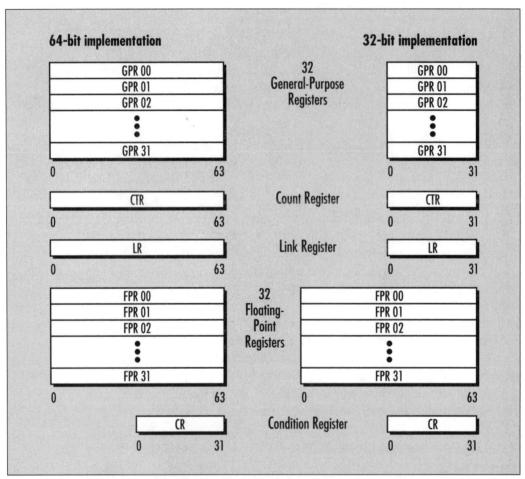

Figure 3. Some Differences and Similarities in the Physical Implementation of a 32-Bit PowerPC Processor and Its 64-Bit Equivalent

32-bit Instructions and Binary Compatibility

In a 64-bit implementation of PowerPC, existing machine instructions
do not change much. Many instructions simply work in *64-bit mode*.
That is, they can manage 64-bit long data and use/generate 64-bit
long addresses. New instructions, which were not implemented in
the previous PowerPC chips, are included to handle 64-bit data.

A 64-bit PowerPC can also work in *32-bit mode*. In this way,
any 32-bit operating system or application that currently runs on
PowerPCs can run unchanged. For example, arithmetic instructions
running in 32-bit mode will operate on the lower half of the CPU
register involved and, in the result, will consider only that half of
the register. 32-bit addresses will be handled in the same way.

Intermixed 32- and 64-bit operation is also supported. Predefined
hardware and software mechanisms allow any combination of the
following to execute:

— 32-bit applications
— 64-bit applications
— 32-bit libraries
— 32-bit operating systems
— 64-bit operating systems
— 64-bit applications calling 32-bit routines

Figure 4 shows a simplified representation of the virtual address space
(that is, the usable memory independent of the size of the physical memory
actually installed in the machine that it's running on) that the PowerPC
architecture can manage in 32-bit and 64-bit modes. As shown, the
32-bit implementation can already address a very large — 2^{52} bytes —
address space. (Refer to Figure 2.) The 64-bit implementation goes up
to 2^{80} bytes (a mind-bogglingly huge number that signifies something
around 1 trillion terabytes, which should suffice in future applications
for quite some time). Other 64-bit architectures currently available
can address a virtual address space that is 2^{64} bytes wide.

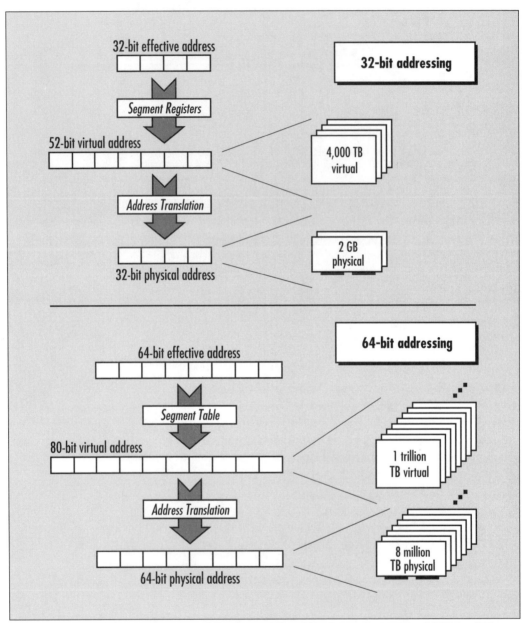

Figure 4. The 32-bit implementation of the PowerPC architecture can manage 4,000 terabytes of virtual address space, thanks to memory segmentation mechanisms. After virtual-to-physical translation, the addressable physical memory is up to 2 gigabytes (GB). A 64-bit implementation of PowerPC supports huge virtual and physical memory.

Buses

In a microprocessor, the *internal buses* are usually defined as the physical interfaces that interconnect the different operational units on the chip. In order to be properly defined as a 64-bit machine, a processor has to be equipped with 64-bit (or larger) internal buses. If these buses were narrower than the word size of the processor, they would become a performance bottleneck, thus making it impossible for the CPU to run at full speed. For this reason, the 64-bit implementations of PowerPC will provide internal bus widths of 64, 128, or more bits.

The same concepts apply to the *system bus* (the bus that typically connects the CPU[s] to the memory subsystem and the I/O controller) and the *I/O bus* (the bus that moves data between the CPU complex and the I/O cards). **Note:** Industry Standard Architecture (ISA), Microchannel, and Peripheral Component Interconnect (PCI) are examples of I/O buses. Some RS/6000 systems today are equipped with 128- or 256-bit wide system buses, and their Microchannel bus moves data in 64-bit wide blocks. On the RS/6000 SMP and Scalable POWERparallel models, the system bus is replaced by a *crossbar switch* that moves data at 1.8 GB per second, the highest speed currently available in the industry. The introduction of 64-bit CPUs will further improve the characteristics and performance of these buses.

The *global* performance of a machine does not depend only on the speed or characteristics of its microprocessor, but derives from a balanced, high performance design in which all components contribute to the processing power of the system complex. As a result, many 32-bit RS/6000 systems today outperform other manufacturers' 64-bit machines on some of the most demanding benchmarks in the UNIX world.

Advantages of a 64-bit Architecture

The following paragraphs detail the advantages that a 64-bit architecture presents: larger programs, larger data, larger files, and larger physical memory.

Larger Programs

As Figure 4 shows, a 64-bit processor can support a much wider
address space when compared to its 32-bit equivalent. This support
means that it is possible to develop much larger and more complex
applications, whereas today's 32-bit applications may have a 4 GB size
limit on some architectures. However, most current applications do
not reach or even approach this limit. In fact, thousands of real-life
applications still run on 16-bit architectures and operating systems.
Future applications, however, will need to go beyond the current
4-GB limit.

Larger Data

Another advantage of 64-bit architectures is their ability to manage
very large amounts of data, possibly in real memory. This ability
greatly simplifies the task for applications that typically handle big
data sets, such as multimedia, statistics, or database applications.

   Although 32-bit environments do not limit most existing applications, the demand for 64-bit capability will increase in the future, as
more powerful and demanding applications are developed. The ability
to handle elementary data larger than 32-bit is also desirable, but many
advanced applications still work on data smaller than 64-bit. For instance, multimedia sound requires 16-bit long data and graphics requires
24- and sometimes 32-bit long data.

Larger Files

A 64-bit environment can easily manage huge files, file systems, and
databases without forcing the application or the operating system to
explicitly handle situations requiring data sets larger than 2 GB. Today's
most sophisticated application enablers, for example, DB2 for AIX,
already support this capability.

   AIX Version 4 itself allows for file systems larger than 2 GB. Advanced
applications using high quality graphics and sound or managing huge

databases (such as weather forecasting, decision support, or virtual reality) are going to become more common, however, and they will greatly benefit from systems that can address and manage such huge amounts of data without forcing the application to worry about limits in data size.

Larger Physical Memory

The physical addresses that a 64-bit chip generates are up to 64 bits long as well. Once again, this size eliminates the 2-GB limit in real memory that all 32-bit architectures share. Actually, many of today's 32-bit systems don't even support as much as 2 GB of real memory and have much lower physical limits. Not many current UNIX installations have that much memory, although hardware providers would love to have more. However, memory requirements of applications grow every year, and, in the future, real memories greater than 2 GB will become more common.

What 64-bit Architectures Are *Not*: Considerations on Hardware Performance

Although 64-bit architectures deliver all the benefits just described (larger programs, data, files, and physical memory), a common misunderstanding is that a 64-bit processor *per se* increases performance. This is not so for the following reasons:

- The larger address space means that larger applications can be developed and executed, without relation to performance.

- The support for larger physical memory gives no advantages if the memory cards are not there. Having large real memories for huge applications will reduce paging, an issue more related to software than to hardware.

- The ability to manage larger disk spaces is a great functional (and programming) advantage if the software is modified to exploit this ability. In itself, 64-bit hardware will not influence performance.

◆ A 64-bit architecture can do 64-bit arithmetic, so if an application needs this function, programmers can avoid writing a library. Again, this ability is an indirect, software-related, performance improvement.

Important characteristics differentiate PowerPC architecture from other processor architectures. First, unlike some of its competitors, PowerPC was *born* as a 64-bit architecture, with 32-bit mode as a functional subset. PowerPC is not an adaptation or "remodeling" of an existing 32-bit architecture. This architectural aspect helps make the transition from 32-bit to 64-bit easier, as does binary compatibility.

Furthermore, 32-bit and 64-bit PowerPC processors are binary compatible with the POWER family of processors. This compatibility not only allows for seamless growth, but also gives UNIX organizations immediate access to the huge number of available applications — as well as more opportunity to protect their investments in current RS/6000 technology.

In other words, it is not enough to be a 64-bit chip in order to be an advanced, functionally rich, high-performance processor. It also takes leading-edge technology and the flexibility, extendability, and capacity for growth that the PowerPC architecture definition provides — today.

AIX and the 64-bit Implementations of PowerPC

By its nature, the PowerPC architecture is an open, extendable design. There is nothing in the chip architecture itself that would affect binary compatibility in migrating across 601, 603, 604, or 64-bit implementations. The PowerPC processor architecture was defined, from the start, as a 64-bit architecture that is a superset of the 32-bit architecture implemented in the 601, 603, and 604 processors. For AIX and the applications that run on AIX, the 64-bit PowerPCs have two independent attributes: They will be faster 32-bit processors, and they will support running a 64-bit environment.

AIX is expected to exploit these attributes separately, initially supporting traditional 32-bit applications on new 64-bit systems. Later, 64-bit systems allowing 64-bit operations are likely through further AIX updates. Significantly, IBM would make no changes to any 32-bit interfaces in this second phase; maintaining binary compatibility for 32-bit applications is the first goal in any 64-bit exploitation IBM would consider. Therefore, UNIX professionals can be confident that IBM will continue to introduce new technology into the RS/6000 and AIX products while protecting users' investments in current systems and applications.

Conclusions

64-bit architectures will introduce a new set of functions and capabilities in the computer systems of the near future. They will overcome traditional architectural limits of 32-bit technology and create opportunities for larger, more sophisticated, and advanced applications. On the other hand, 32-bit systems have quite a ways to go before they are fully exploited, and today, very few applications exploiting 64-bit environments are available.

In this transition, the requirements of users and business partners will drive IBM's strategy. The IBM RISC System/6000 Division is rolling out a plan dictated by users' demands and will develop the plan by cooperating with software vendors that want to provide 64-bit applications and solutions. Binary compatibility, application availability, and the capacity for growth will drive IBM's efforts.

Acknowledgments

As author, I am the only person to be blamed for errors, inaccuracies, or incompleteness. This article, however, resulted from a team effort to provide me with material on 64-bit architectures. In particular, my thanks go to Jane Bebar, Fred Bothwell, Kaivalya Dixit, Robert Henson, Ernesto Hofmann, John Kingman, Francesco Lacapra, William O'Leary, Luca Pistolesi, and Bill Smith. They helped me prepare the article, reviewed its first drafts, and provided invaluable feedback and comments.

The Industry Initiative on 64-Bit Computing

As we move toward the millennium, enterprise users' demands
for faster, larger systems have already begun to push computing
to the next level — to the 64-bit level. To prepare for 64-bit computing, the computer industry must begin to build support and
to collaborate *now*.

On August 15, 1995, computer industry leaders supporting
current architectures — including Intel's Pentium, Hewlett-Packard's
PA-RISC, Digital's Alpha, IBM's PowerPC, Silicon Graphics/MIPS
RISC, and Sun's SPARC — endorsed the development of a common
64-bit UNIX API. Coupled with a common 64-bit data representation model in the C programming language, the API set will
support supercomputers, enterprise and workgroup servers,
workstations, and networks.

Because widely accepted industry standards at the 64-bit level do
not exist, the initiative gives industry leaders — UNIX suppliers,
software application developers, and computer manufacturers —
a unique opportunity to support an efficient 64-bit UNIX model.
By building from existing 32-bit APIs, the 64-bit API will also be
upward-compatible with 32-bit applications.

The 64-bit UNIX API specification, when accepted by the X/Open
standards body, will comply with and track existing standards such
as XPG 4.2 (*a.k.a.* Spec 1170), Portable Operating System Interface
for UNIX (POSIX), System V Interface Definition (SVID), Common
Desktop Environment (CDE), and X-Windows. By including the
leading industry APIs, system utilities, and network computing
interfaces, the initiative will ensure that applications are robust
enough to access necessary services.

Significantly, this initiative does not propose developing a single
product to run on one company's platform, but to establish specifications that allow applications to run on any complying UNIX

system. In addition, the initiative should reduce the variables and complexities faced by software developers as well as simplifying decision-making for IT managers.

A major participant in the open systems and UNIX "culture," IBM has long sought to collaborate with others on open standards, even while it competes vigorously with them. IBM's goal is to improve communications in heterogeneous environments and to ease integration of systems and devices in a network-centric world — a world in which every user who wishes to, can participate.

As one of IBM's major operating environments, AIX runs on hundreds of thousands of systems worldwide and is recognized for its scalability, systems management, ease of use, and other proven capabilities. IBM will continue to be involved in the evolution of the UNIX operating system.

In that spirit, AIX currently supports a wide and growing range of existing UNIX middleware and applications. And it is in that same spirit of collaboration that IBM has joined in the 64-bit initiative.

Clearly, such an effort is needed. There is, after all, no lack of demand from customers for more powerful, flexible systems and scalable applications. And demand is growing for such emerging applications as web servers, data mining, collaborative computing, video servers, and digital libraries — all of which would be facilitated by 64-bit addressability.

The initiative IBM has joined is simply the next logical step, one that will help meet users' growing expectations while protecting their investments in 32-bit applications. The 64-bit specification will be submitted to X/Open for adoption, building industry support and helping to ensure that applications can be ready to exploit the 64-bit functionality when this capability becomes a reality.

Dr. Irving Wladawsky-Berger

Dr. Irving Wladawsky-Berger, is general manager of the new IBM Internet division. He wrote this chapter while still serving as general manager of IBM's RISC System/6000 division, which was combined with the POWER Parallel division in June 1995. Earlier, Wladawsky-Berger was instrumental in initiating IBM's System/390 microprocessor and parallel technology efforts. Wladawsky-Berger joined IBM in 1970 at the Thomas J. Watson Research Center in Yorktown Heights, NY. He holds master's and doctor's degrees from the University of Chicago, is a member of the Fermilab Board of Overseers, and served on the Computer Sciences and Telecommunications Board of the National Research Council.

Technical Brief: Parallel Computing: Scalability at An Affordable Price

By Dr. Irving Wladawsky-Berger

This chapter provides a general overview of the four alternative technologies for delivering highly scalable computing systems. These technologies — designed to meet users' growing demands for increased processing power — include large uniprocessors, client/server, symmetric multiprocessors, and parallel systems. The chapter also highlights IBM development efforts in each of these areas.

Demand for scalable systems is growing. Stated simply, a scalable system is one that permits the addition of processing power, storage, memory, input/output (I/O), and connectivity with relative ease, so user organizations can deploy larger, more complex, more sophisticated applications; exploit constantly growing databases; and make both available to increasing numbers of users through very high bandwidth networks.

The building blocks of scalable systems are readily available in the form of technologies that are comparatively inexpensive and getting more so. These technologies include complementary metal oxide semiconductor-based microprocessors, memories, disk and optical storage, tapes, and I/O and communications adapters. Building parallel systems with these technologies can provide scalability almost without limit at an attractive price and thus represents the most rational way to leverage these technologies to solve large problems.

Since scalability is so fundamental to the solution of large problems, the alternatives merit discussion. There are at least four ways to provide scalable systems. This chapter will present a brief technical overview of each method available.

CLIENT/SERVER

Most vendors of PCs, workstations, and their related servers advocate open, distributed, client/server configurations as a way to scale. Essentially, this method involves linking servers and clients through local area networks (LANs) or wide area networks (WANs), a configuration that can be scaled by adding systems. Building very large client/server configurations involves considerable support and management cost after the initial hardware and software investment. The evidence suggests that client/server systems perform very well in support of personal, departmental, and midsize applications. But scaling by adding more systems presents a degree of complexity that is only now becoming apparent.

As client/server systems become larger and more complex, adding many more clients and distributed servers connected to larger centralized servers, and as the notion of the network-as-computer takes hold, the issue of systems management will be even more critical. Fortunately, tools like SystemView exist for managing these large configurations.

LARGER UNIPROCESSORS

Technically, the simplest way to provide scalability is to build ever larger and faster uniprocessors. Processor speed can be increased with unique technologies — bipolar or gallium arsenide, for example. Systems can also be made faster using highly sophisticated architectures, either alone or in combination with unique technologies. The advantage of scaling uniprocessors is that the software remains the same — it simply runs on a faster processor.

While technologically elegant, the price/performance of this alternative compares poorly with its chief competition — the high-volume, low-cost microprocessors used in personal computers and workstations. This competitive disadvantage of uniprocessors based on unique technology is why IBM, and most other computer manufacturers, are beginning to use microprocessors based on complementary metal oxide semiconductor (CMOS) technology.

Though today's CMOS microprocessors are less expensive than today's unique bipolar systems, they are slower. Still, their performance is growing much faster and likely will achieve the level of IBM's System/390 (S/390) bipolar processors in 1997.

SYMMETRIC MULTIPROCESSORS

One can also scale by integrating multiple uniprocessors into a single system in which they share resources like memory, I/O, the operating system, and application software. Having one of each resource makes a symmetric multiprocessor (SMP) system relatively easy to program and manage. In addition, the SMP will run essentially the same software as the uniprocessor, though it may have to be modified to remove bottlenecks that the faster multiprocessor could expose.

IBM has developed System/390 bipolar SMPs for a number of years by integrating several uniprocessors into a single system referred to as a "tightly coupled multiprocessor." In its ability to get extremely efficient performance from 6-, 8-, and 10-way SMP configurations, the System/390 is in a class by itself. With the adaptation of the AIX operating system to support them, SMPs have become part of the RISC System/6000 (RS/6000) family. Likewise, SMPs have been added to IBM's PC Server line, while the AS/400 incorporated them into its product line some time ago.

IBM's UNIX competitors have been offering SMPs for several years. Now, key middleware (*e.g.*, databases and transaction managers) and applications are being adapted to the RS/6000's SMP models. As a result, a considerable volume of software is already available for these configurations. Nevertheless, UNIX systems have substantial work to do before they can approach the efficiencies of the S/390 in supporting SMPs.

SMP systems can scale more cost-effectively than uniprocessors. However, as capacity is added to SMPs, the shared memory, I/O, and software that are their main advantage in terms of programming and management become bottlenecks. Each additional microprocessor contends for finite resources, and increasing amounts of capacity have to be devoted to overhead (*i.e.*, managing memory, I/O, etc.). This situation has been called "the Von Neumann bottleneck" after the father of modern computing.

The Von Neumann bottleneck is the technological equivalent of the law of diminishing returns. Ideally, the addition of a second processor should double performance, while a third triples it, and so on. As a practical matter, achieving a performance improvement of 1.7 to 1.9 from the addition of a second processor is cause for celebration. As more processors are added, the losses to contention and overhead accelerate. More capacity is devoted to overhead and contention, less to productive work.

Scaling SMP systems well beyond four processors requires a good deal of innovative design and exquisite tuning — in short, it's very hard work. It can be done, but there is a point where the return is simply not worth the effort. SMPs will always be preferable for moderate scalability, but not beyond. This fact is the reason why S/390 is not going beyond a tightly coupled 10-way bipolar system and why IBM's large systems competitors are unlikely to go very much beyond that.

PARALLEL SYSTEMS

When multiple processors are connected to each other by a high-performance interconnect mechanism — and each processor has its own memory, its own I/O configuration, and its own copy of the operating system — far higher levels of scalability are achievable. Indeed, such systems become almost infinitely scalable because the incremental processor does not increase contention for resources; it comes with all it needs to do productive work. In addition, the interconnect mechanism can keep pace as processors are added, so the hardware is seldom a bottleneck. The resulting configuration offers the prospect of systems with processors by the hundreds — even thousands — communicating through huge bandwidths with each other and with trillions of bytes of storage.

Parallel systems present two major challenges:

◆ "Parallelizing" the application software and all the key databases, transactions, and storage managers (in short, all the software that falls into the category of middleware)

◆ "Efficiently" managing a system that is composed of multiple copies of everything

IBM has instituted two major parallel computing efforts. In both the S/390 and POWERparallel environments, the adaptation of software is well underway, and IBM is applying the experience gained in three decades of managing large, complex systems to these scalable, parallel systems.

System/390 Parallel Systems

The System/390 Parallel Sysplex is designed to exploit IBM's investment in the MVS operating system and related system software — such as CICS, IMS, DB2, and VSAM — and to make it possible for user organizations to migrate their huge installed base of S/390 applications that currently run on IBM mainframes. The S/390 Parallel Sysplex Architecture makes it possible for multiple MVS systems to cooperate in parallel by sharing information through a coupling facility at very high speeds.

Apart from the raw processing power this architecture permits, the Parallel Sysplex provides user organizations with several other advantages that make it attractive even before SMPs reach the limits of scalability:

◆ They can add capacity — either bipolar or CMOS-based — in modest or large increments, from a single 13 MIPS "engine" to clusters of systems delivering thousands of MIPS.

◆ Most existing applications can function within the architecture without being rewritten, so software investments are protected.

◆ The system will run 24 hours a day, 7 days a week.

◆ It has the ability to manage many systems as a single system, reducing the complexity, resources, and costs users face.

Extensive efforts are underway at IBM software laboratories and among independent software vendors to transform MVS into an effective parallel system that fully exploits the scalable S/390 architecture while providing outstanding systems management. IBM expects that most S/390 applications will be able to take advantage of this work and the architecture and migrate to S/390 parallel systems with minimal difficulty.

However, no one would suggest that the transition to the Parallel Sysplex environment is always totally painless. For one thing, user organizations must be running the latest releases of the operating system software, so a software upgrade or migration will often be necessary. In addition, scaling applications and databases usually entails unforeseen complexities irrespective of the underlying architecture.

Scalable POWERparallel Systems

Just as the System/390's parallel architecture leverages the huge MVS installed base, so the Scalable POWERparallel (SP) systems are designed to exploit all the energies building in UNIX and RISC systems, especially in IBM's own RS/6000 family.

UNIX is an established force in the market for workstations; mid-range servers; distributed, client/server computing; and scientific supercomputing. Apart from scientific supercomputing, the development of UNIX applications is concentrated on low-end and midrange systems. Thus, the task of a parallel UNIX system is to scale up from the desktop and midrange. Since IBM's SP uses the POWER/PowerPC microprocessors and the AIX operating system, it runs virtually all applications written for the RS/6000 and readily supports applications built for other UNIX systems.

The primary objective in the commercial sphere is directed toward "parallelizing" applications and middleware, the layer of software that supports applications. IBM's own labs are adapting such software as DB2/6000 and CICS/6000 to support scalable, parallel UNIX systems. And independent software vendors like Oracle, Tuxedo, Sybase, Informix, and SAP are doing likewise with their products. For most, this represents their first effort to support large, scalable UNIX systems. Some applications, like decision support, are already available on the SP platform; others, like high-performance transaction processing, will require more time to mature in the marketplace.

Considerable activity is underway to produce scalable software for the SP platform. However, this product is new, both to users and to developers. As a result, it will take some time before a critical mass of scalable software is achieved.

The exception to "scaling from below" is scientific supercomputing. Most supercomputer users adopted UNIX several years ago, and high-performance vector supercomputers have supported many large technical applications. For this class of applications at the high end, POWER Parallel's task is to enable existing supercomputing applications written for vector-assisted SMPs to run on the SP platform and to provide tools and compilers so new parallel supercomputing applications can be written. This ongoing effort has produced many applications with many more to come.

SUMMARY

For IBM, the S/390 parallel and POWER Parallel scalable computing efforts represent important near- and long-term opportunities and critical, strategic investments. The days of bipolar systems are ultimately numbered. Even Hitachi will be buying IBM's S/390 CMOS microprocessors for its systems. In fact, Hitachi's recently announced new system is a combination of bipolar and CMOS technology.

As base technologies continue to take on the characteristics of "commodities," they will increase the importance of scalable computing systems that can use them to provide very large systems at affordable prices. And as new network-centric applications emerge, supporting huge multimedia information libraries and affording access to millions of users around the world, scalable, microprocessor-based systems will be the servers of choice in the network. Given its market leadership and its core competencies in designing large systems and solving large problems, IBM is well positioned to meet user organizations' needs in this arena.

The following items are trademarks, registered trademarks, or service marks of their respective companies or organizations:

AIX, AIX/6000, AIX DCE Threads/6000, AIX/ESA, AIXwindows, AIX Xstation Manager/6000, AIX Performance Toolbox/6000 (PTX/6000), AIX Performance Aide/6000 (PAIDE/6000), APPN, AnyNet, Customer Information Control System/6000 (CICS/6000), Distributed Relational Database Architecture (DRDA), Enterprise System/9000 (ES/9000), FastService, geoManager, geoManager/6000, High Availability Cluster Multi-Processing/6000 (HACMP/6000), IBM, InfoCrafter, InfoExplorer, LoadLeveler, 9333 High-Performance Disk Drive Subsystem, 9076 Scalable POWERparallel SP1, SP2, Micro Channel, MVS, MVS/ESA, NetView, NetView/6000, 3995 Optical Library Dataserver, Operating System/2, OS/2, POWER Architecture, PowerPC, POWERserver, POWERstation, Presentation Manager, Personal System/2, PS/2, RISC System/6000, RS/6000, Software Development Environment/6000 (SDE/6000), Systems Application Architecture (SAA), Systems Network Architecture (SNA), SQL/DS, THINK, ThinkPad, Token-Ring, Workplace Shell, 3090, VM, VTAM, and X25Net; all of International Business Machines Corporation

ANSI, American National Standards Institute

Apple, Macintosh, Power Mac, AppleTalk, AppleShare, QuickTime, QuickDraw GX, TrueType, System 7, and AppleSearch; all of Apple Computer, Inc.

AT&T and C++, both of AT&T Corporation

Banyan and VINES, both of Banyan Systems Incorporated

CADAM and CATIA, both of Dassault Systems

Cheyenne, Cheyenne, Inc.

CLARiiON and ArrayGUIde, both of Data General Corporation

COMDEX, Interface Group, Inc.

DEC, DECNET, ULTRIX, VAX, and VMS; all of Digital Equipment Corporation

EasySpooler, Seay Systems

Elan License Manager and SoftWatch, both of Elan Computer Group

Encina and AFS, both of Transarc Corp.

Ethernet, Xerox Corp.

Excalibur XRS, MediaScript, Adaptive Pattern Recognition Processing, APRP, and Excalibur TRS; all of Excalibur Technologies Corporation

Excel and Lotus 1-2-3, both of Lotus Development Corp.

FLEXlm, FLEXadmin, and FLEXwrap; all of Globetrotter Software

GigaRAID, RMU, and ANDATACO; all of ANDATACO Corp.

HDS, Human Designed Systems, Inc.

Hewlett-Packard, Network Computing System, and HP-UX; all of Hewlett-Packard Corp.

Informix, Informix

Innovus Networker, Innovus, Inc.

Internet, Internet, Inc.

InSoft and Communique!, both of InSoft, Inc.

ISO, Open System Interconnect, and OSI; all of International Standards Organization

Legato Networker, Legato Systems, Inc.

Locus, PC-Interface, and PC-Interface Plus; all of Locus Computing Corporation

Magic Software Enterprises, Magic Software Enterprises, Inc.

MIPS, MIPS Computer Corporation

MONITROL and Kinetix, both of Hilco Technologies

Motorola, Motorola, Inc.

Open M, Enterprise Server Solution, Bullet Proof Database, and Distributed Cache Protocol; all of InterSystems Corporation

Open M/SQL, InterSystems Corporation

Open Software Foundation, Distributed Computing Environment, DCE, OSF, OSF/1, Motif, and OSF/Motif; all of the Open Software Foundation Inc.

Oracle, Oracle Corp.

PacerTerm, PacerShare, and PacerPrint; all of Pacer Software, Inc.

PeopleSoft, PeopleCode, PeopleTalk, PeopleTools, and PS/nVision; all of PeopleSoft, Inc.

POSIX and IEEE, both of the Institute of Electrical and Electronics Engineers

PowerOpen, PowerOpen Association, Inc.

Prestoserve, Legato Systems, Inc.

Red Brick and Red Brick Warehouse VPT, both of Red Brick Systems

REEL Manager, REELlibrarian, REELbackup, REELaccess, and REELexchange; all of Software Clearing House

SCO, The Santa Cruz Operation, Inc.

Silicon Graphics and IRIX, both of Silicon Graphics Corp.

SmartStream, Dun & Bradstreet Software Services, Inc.

Software Professionals, Inc. and ENlighten, both of Software Professionals, Inc.

SPEC, SPECint92, and SPECfp92; all of the System Performance Evaluation Corp.

Sun, SunOS, Solaris, Sun Microsystems, ToolTalk, NFS, and SunSoft; all of Sun Microsystems, Inc.

Sybase, Sybase Inc.

TPC-C, Transaction Processing Performance Council

UniDirect, UniDirect Corporation

Univel, Univel

UNIX and OPEN LOOK, UNIX System Laboratories, Inc., a wholly-owned subsidiary of Novell, Inc. (UNIX is licensed exclusively by X/Open Company Limited)

UnixWare, Novell, Inc.

UNI/XT, THOMSON-CSF

Windows, Windows NT, LAN Manager, Win32, Windows for Workgroups, and Microsoft; all of Microsoft Corporation

X/Open, the "X" device, XPG3, and XPG4; all of X/Open Company Limited

X Window System and Kerberos, both of Massachusetts Institute of Technology

Index